I Married a Greek

Enjoy!

~Acknowledgements~

Special thanks to these individuals and organizations for helping edit and prepare this book for publication:

Anne Estes
Cathy Haralson
Shere Goo
Mill Valley Graphics

www.imarriedagreek.net

I Married a Greek

Selected Stories

By Patricia F. Mouille

Order this book online at www.imarriedagreek.net

Most Trafford titles are also available at major online book retailers.

Note for Librarians: A cataloguing record for this book is available from Library and Archives Canada at www.collectionscanada.ca/amicus/index-e.html

Printed in Victoria, BC, Canada.

ISBN: 978-1-4251-8680-7

We at Trafford believe that it is the responsibility of us all, as both individuals and corporations, to make choices that are environmentally and socially sound. You, in turn, are supporting this responsible conduct each time you purchase a Trafford book, or make use of our publishing services. To find out how you are helping, please visit www.trafford.com/responsiblepublishing.html

Our mission is to efficiently provide the world's finest, most comprehensive book publishing service, enabling every author to experience success. To find out how to publish your book, your way, and have it available worldwide, visit us online at www.trafford.com/10510

www.trafford.com

North America & international
toll-free: 1 888 232 4444 (USA & Canada)
phone: 250 383 6864 • fax: 250 383 6804
email: info@trafford.com

The United Kingdom & Europe
phone: +44 (0)1865 487 395 • local rate: 0845 230 9601
facsimile: +44 (0)1865 481 507 • email: info.uk@trafford.com

10 9 8 7 6 5 4

To the Greek who married me

(don't worry dear, I changed the family's names)

Contents

Leonidis

My poor darling Kostas, caught up in pain and sadness, was expressing it in a higher than usual decibel, albeit monotone, rampage. This was a man, who although he had known of his brother's coming demise, had not experienced the hopelessness of his terminal illness. He had not seen for himself the steps down declining health to death's door until now. A speck of a man lay before him, his body lifeless with exception to the tubes entering and leaving his body. Two eyes and a nose on a colorless, hollowed face. Chest and shoulders once broad, now gone, lost forever. Color faded, yellowed over, a whitening as in the sheets. Good bye sweet brother, so close, right there, a man no more; spirit ready to rise away from the body and into the heaven to enjoin spirit with their father.

Yet, as Kostas walked out the front door and as its steel bar gate clanked closed behind him, he held his head high, shoulders erect, walking tall as is his usual manner. He strolled seemingly confident, beside his sister in law, Chara, as they jointly surveyed the potted flowering plants so arranged on the sidewalk and steps by the village street merchant. He called to me, glad to be able to change the subject so quickly from pain to pleasure. "Come here Baby, pick out one plant for Mama." And so I opened the door and joined him pretending not to recognize his strife, the utter sadness hidden beneath the chore of selecting the proper begonia. Equal time was spent figuring out that it was improper to transport the plant in the trunk, even though we knew it was not in the best interest of Anatolios' mental health to tote it in the passenger cabin and therefore risk leaf and or soil droppings. But Kostas offered to hold the plant between his legs in the front seat during travel, which for anyone who knows him, knows this is far from an occupation he might otherwise undertake.

And so it was. Anatolios accelerated out of this particular neighborhood, one tree lined and otherwise colorful, now bleak and ruined, and into the hustle-bustle traffic of Thessaloniki. Horns honking, drivers hollering and a dog chasing and barking at a motorbike wagon with three gypsies in the back. Finally we passed out of this city, Thessaloniki, which usually holds great and powerful memory and meaning to my husband, always a favored stop in our annual tour of Greece, now forever to hold a heart-wrenching episode in our travels.

But it was the freeway ride that would punch Kostas first, forcing him to expel the fear, to piss away the energy of having hopelessness in one's midst. It was all in Greek. Loud and sure, a eulogy to his brother, their family, their strength. Mama, the reference to father. The blessings of children, long and otherwise healthy lives. Heaving words without breath. I grabbed his neck and shoulders from behind and felt the passion stirring within him. The heart pumping enough blood for the whole car full. His brother Anatolios, driving without words but seemingly holding a little bit of satisfaction in seeing at least one other brother experiencing and, oh yes, letting go the same kind of brotherly love and sadness.

And Chara, behind her husband, next to me agreeing with Kostas. Affirming every statement of fact. Praising his words, testifying to their truth. On and on, how compelling and after at least 15 kilometers of ranting he began to release his sobbing on to me. Through his neck and shoulders, on to my fingers, hands to arms, chest to neck and to my head, his sorrow and pain and sadness. My eyes swelled, my nose and ducts began to shed. I bit my lips, looked outside as I wept. His sadness became mine. I cried his tears away and on and on. There was no way I could keep Chara from seeing, but neither brother could. The duration was nearly another 15 kilometers, or twelve minutes and then the subject gently changed to lunch and sleep and other things.

Kostas had rid himself of any more displays of open wounds. He recognized that it was so much more than chance that Leonidis would leave us all within our summer stay in Greece. That he, Kostas, would be expected to be the family pillar, emotionless, the one that would set the particulars, outline the provisions, shake out the loose, tighten the weak. Call the other three brothers. Inform them on the truth. Advise. Stir. Compose. And more than anything else, carry the peace, if at all possible, to the mother of these six sons, the firstborn who now will be the first to die. Amen.

Greeks speak loudly. Mostly quickly. Let me say that again, Greeks speak loudly and mostly quickly, and then when the final issue or point of authority comes to head, the two principal speakers slow down and enunciate on a level as if whispering to a child in church.

It's been four days now since Kostas and I arrived. Yesterday there was a caravan of family arriving in Thessaloniki for a surgery of which we all know now was hopeless. The surgeons had opened him up, once again, and the cancer was spread well beyond the organs and now into the system. The drugs had brought him into a short coma then into a spell of delirium and most of the visitors had left for home to prepare for the final destination by early afternoon.

At 7:45 on Friday morning Mama had rapped gently on the

glass of our door and sung out, "Kostaaaaas."

"Yes, Mama". He sat on the side of the bed, wiping the sleep from his eyes.

"Get up Baby, get me my breakfast."

And so I got up and dressed and rode the elevator downstairs. There she had already made them. The lukmathes, a Greek fashion between a pancake and a donut, were carefully sugared and cinnamoned and placed neatly in the bowl.

"Kametheis kala koriche?" Which translated is, "Sleep well, Doll?"

"Nei, Mama Nei." (Yes I had.) And I lied.

The water for my tea had also been made ready. I took out the banana and strawberry and put them in place. Mixed and shook up the frappé. Poured the juice, took out the fancy forks and that's the breakfast tray. Mama opened the gate with a creak and I scaled the stairs with tray in tow to the top floor.

Kostas was already on the balcony dressed and shaven. He complained that it was too early for lukmathes, that Mama shouldn't have done that, yet he ate them with peaceful vigor. I sipped hot tea after eating my bowl of fruit. The chamomile caused my face to flush and I pardoned myself back to bed. Six minutes later Kostas kissed me goodbye and I could see the face of prepared emotional let down as he whisked off to the city.

I had been sick with a cold the night before. Heavy nose run and cough I believe I caught in the bus at the Munich airport from a fellow who was constantly coughing next to us most of the way to Greece. And so I slept until eleven, got up and cleared the tray outside and gathered my things for a shower.

I found Mama wasn't in good condition, again. She had been crying and probably praying for that miracle of miracles. Leonidis' grown (Down syndrome) son, Dionysius was outside the kitchen window on the balcony seemingly well entertained with a magazine. Laughing or at least musing out loud.

I walked down the hall and turned on the switch to heat my shower water. That usually takes ten minutes, so I returned to the living room. I looked on the table for my People magazine with Erica Kane on the cover. It was misplaced. Dionysius had it and was busying himself with the pictures without care of character or celebrity.

He was clearly waiting. The night before he had posed the question straight forward to his uncle, "Tomorrow the doctors will work on my father. Uncle Kostas, will he be alright?"

To which Kostas replied, "Only God knows, Dionysius, only

God knows." Both swallowed deeply and gazed out away from each other.

He understood more than most thought. He and his father were constant companions. His dad had made sure he was always clean, fresh and well fed. He sent him out on small errands which he knew were not beyond his limited, but well-tested, capabilities. The son watched his father for cues, imitated his actions and even gestures. Occasionally, Dionysius refused orders and his father would give in, because after all, he didn't want to ask too much of this, his only son.

And now the father who alone had brought this retarded son into manhood; who had lost his first wife, Dionysius's mother, to a brain tumor some 12 years before, had married unsuccessfully 7 years after that. Then, just before Christmas, had landed a new bride with whom he had hoped he would share his and his son's remaining years together, succumbed to cancer himself. So what would become of Dionysius, this boy man? Would the family take him away? Most importantly to Dionysius, would his father survive and what if, if not?

I went in for my shower, washed and conditioned my hair. I heard the downstairs buzzer. By the time I came out Dionysius was out of sight and Mama sat chattering with Catalin, a kind lady who is married to my husband's first cousin, also named Kostas after their grandfather. Catalin had brought a homemade cake as offering. We touched hands, kissed from side to side and I made my apologies for the wet hair and went upstairs via elevator. I returned a moment later with an American scene potholder. In my broken Greek I said, "All the years we have had cake by Catalin, and here is a small souvenir from America for your kitchen." She insisted it wasn't necessary and I nodded and waved myself away upstairs to comb out my hair. After that I spent the next 2 hours reading, with my feet in a tub of cool water.

When I came downstairs just before 2 pm, Dionysius and Mama sat there in the living room together. Mama said, "Perimino, Patricia." Which translates to "We are waiting." The phone rang and Dionysius leaned forward in complete anticipation. It was not word from the hospital. I set the table and said I'd be upstairs. When the buzzer downstairs rang just about 3 pm I recognized from the pattern and duration it was Kostas. I ran downstairs. Dionysius had already eaten and was undressed in the extra room, prepared to take his afternoon nap. He quickly dressed and sat across the table from Kostas holding on to his every word, waiting to hear about his dad. It was evident that Kostas was not going to be the one who told, at least not then, either Dionysius or Mama that the end was very near. We ate and made small chatter. By 4pm Anatolios came by and told Dionysius to get ready to go to Litohoro to see his sister and the kids. He happily obliged.

Mama is pretty much inconsolable. She enters fits of crying, holding her mouth to one side of her face. Rocking in sadness. Looking out into thin air with red swollen eyes. "Leonidis" she cries. It's never supposed to be the child before the mother. He 65 and she, at least this time last year, a young 84.

Most recently she cried about how he never wanted anything. "You want a banana, Leonidis?"

"No, Mama," he'd say.

"Portocoloda?"

"No, Mama." He didn't want orange juice.

He never wanted anything. It was all okay with him. He never wanted anything. With rare exception from the time his first wife died and then with lapses and special reasons, he usually dined with Mama. He'd shop for her. She never leaves the home nowadays except for special family outings to a restaurant. So every morning he'd bring her the food she was to cook and or eat, the things needed that day from meat to fish to vegetables, bread, milk, yogurt, eggs, shampoo, detergent, toilet paper and all the rest. He bought it all. He brought it home. He and Dionysius ate it with her, kept company and watched over her.

A long time ago Mama's house was on the ground level. She

had had a yard and a garden and a porch. But Katerini had grown up over the years and four to six story apartments with ground floor storefronts are commonplace.

So the boys, that is, her six sons, pooled their resources, some twenty years ago and rebuilt the home. Now it's four stories high. Downstairs is Leonidis' carpet store and by its side another storefront that once housed Lukas, the fourth son's architecture office. It's now vacant as Lukas has moved back to Washington State to be with his American wife and grown sons.

On the second floor is Anatolios, Mama's second son's doctor's offices. The clinic is not so busy as he is pretty much retired now, but he is nonetheless, the provisional son. He pretty much pays for the upkeep of the building, which is no small task. He frets, a worrisome fellow, but he's a Mama's boy. Acting the sergeant, his wife, Chara is a secondary school educator with an iron fist, a bit of a loose tongue but a good heart. Anatolios has coffee every morning with his mother and although mostly he dines at his own home is constantly munching at Mama's.

The third floor is Mama's house. It's a two-bedroom, one-bath home with sliding glass wood framed doors. The place is tastefully outfitted in fine wood with many built-in features. Her kitchen is small and it's certain that if she had been part of the planning process, the oversized dining room would have made way for more of a kitchen. Nonetheless it's her domain. The furniture is all old world with clawed feet and curved wood. There are doilies everywhere along with plastic flowers and loads of little knick knacks and collectibles she's been gifted over time. Photographs, lots of photographs, and a big hand-painted portrait of her deceased husband, their deceased father, Thanos Petras, sits above eye level and without question watches over this home.

On the fourth floor are the guest quarters, which is no more than a good sized bedroom with a hallway separating it from a half bath. There's a full window in the hallway, making discreet passage from the bed to washroom impossible.

The balcony, or should I call it a terrace or plateau, is pretty spectacular. You can see all around the city. From one end you can even glimpse Mt. Olympus, home of the Gods. Mama's green thumb is also very evident as there are no less than, let me count, 59 potted, mostly flowering plants. A nice iron dining set with a big, sturdy cloth umbrella is the centerpiece, so truly "our balcony" is the family hang out, at least while we are in town.

In the middle of the hallway and in fact, the whole building, is the marble spiral staircase polished clean each week by Mama's house help. Midway from our floor to Mama's begins a plant per stair, which because of the spiral, makes the stepping down a test of agility. Thank goodness for the elevator beside it, which stops at each floor.

Outside Mama's beautiful multi-wood front door leading upstairs is the creaky gate. The noise it makes insures that anyone above knows company is on its way. Unless, of course, the elevator is used.

OH SHIT, he's gone. What do I do? Nothing, what can I do? I'm not quite sure how we learned, but Kostas is downstairs with an official looking paper that he must have just been served at the front door. But first Anatolios had called. Kostas had a towel wrapped around him as he had already undressed to lay down to his afternoon nap. Monday 4:24 pm. That's June 14th. He's gone.

Mama had such a frightful look on her face. Ordering me to leave the kitchen, leaving the dishes that are my job, undone. Now I'm in the way. Dispensable. He's gone. My husband's brother, his mother's son. Adara, Anatolios' daughter, had already come by and was holding Mama in the kitchen, or rather they were holding each other. She must have just left her father who has to be as bad off as Mama, for they were both crying last night so full of pity for themselves.

I close my eyes and, "Yasou Nidis." I'm upstairs by myself and

I will stay there until I am called for. I don't know what to do. My poor dear husband, so full of resolve before. To protect, preserve and now what? He will be the one to make the calls; tell the other brothers. Hear them gasp; hear them cry. The brothers.

There are six brothers, at least there were. Leonidis was the oldest at sixty-five. Anatolios, the doctor, was a year and a half younger. He supports two kids in college: Adara who is supposedly finishing up a med tech degree in Scotland, and Thanos who is sessions away from a law degree in the military.

My dear Kostas, will be 61 in November and then a year and a half apart, is Lukas, the architect living in Washington State where he went to college and met his wife Susan. They have two grown sons, Thanos and Anatolios. Next son is Alexis, or Alex, a singer/entertainer who makes a pretty decent living working the island circuit.

Nightclubs are big in the tourist islands of Crete, Rhodos and such keep him busy. Alexis is married to Phoebe, whose parents live just outside Katerini. They live in Athens with their two grown children, Adara and Thanos.

And last but not least, the baby son is Dionysius who is fifty-two and married to Vasiliki, a school chum. Interestingly enough they spent nearly 30 years apart after first meeting and falling in love at school. Each then marrying others, then splitting, in order to get back together. She has two sons from her first marriage and Dionysius has three children Chole, Thanos and Maria with his first wife, Philothea. They live just outside San Francisco.

I'm not sure how this is done in Greece. I understand the body is laid out for viewing for a day then I think the services and burial are supposed to occur within twenty four hours. I know there's no party like the Catholics do. Oh my God, this is going to be awful...

I'm sitting at the top of the stairs and can just slightly hear what's going on within. Mama's crying. Someone, another one has just rung the buzzer downstairs and is on their way up. Now Anatolios is speaking at a very high decibel, I presume to hide the pain. Unfortunately motor bikes outside with engines rumbling are drowning out his voice. I can't hear Mama's cry anymore. Anatolios, I'm sure, is on the phone because he just said, "Yes, yes Kostas is here," and "Yes, Mama is here too." I'm sure whoever it is, they would like to speak to her but now is not the best time to talk.

I have calmed now. The tears are dry. The fear has subsided. It is now the family, all the family. God help us all.

Chara rang the buzzer down stairs. I hear Kostas tell

Anatolios, "Yinaka," which means your woman, your wife. Anatolios buzzed his wife in. As she came out of the elevator, she went immediately to Mama's side. Now her voice is raised. She's speaking loudly and forcibly, talking to Mama in an attempt to calm. Mama is moaning loudly in pain, crying, suffering.

Now the gate creaks. It is Kostas accelerating up the stairs with a glass of juice. I throw my journal under the table. He sees me and asks for the aspirin. I touch his arm and hold and say, "I'm here Baby."

"Yes, I know. Now go outside." I don't.

Kostas went back downstairs. The phone rings. Kostas says "Nei, Nei Nei." (Yes, yes, Yes.) "Kostas. Kostas Petras." He then orders Chara to get Anatolios who is now on the cell phone giving thorough orders, number specifications and such. As minutes turn into an hour and then into two, tension continues to fill the air downstairs.

Mama has lost a lot of weight since her son has become ill. The last time she needed to wear black she was a few sizes bigger so I hear women talking, rustling about in her closet and back bedroom looking for something black for her to wear that's not so voluminous. Kostas comes upstairs and asks me to come down and make him some frappé-ice coffee. Since the last time he was upstairs, I changed from my summer clothes of white shorts and sleeveless blue shirt to my black jeans and dark blue jersey—dark, all dark.

Kostas' first cousin, Dora walks by. Her face is puffy and swollen. Her eyes red and very sad. I touch her forearm and hold on for a second or two. And there is Catalin, her sister-in-law. Weeping and sobbing, looking out a window with swollen strawberry eyes, holding a fist up under her honking rose nose.

So this is the beginning. The other women are fussing inside the back room now. I finish my duty making coffee and feeling out of place, retreat back upstairs.

Nearly another hour passes before Kostas summons me again. I oblige and hop in the elevator. Downstairs is quiet. He and Anatolios are straightening themselves up, getting ready for some waiting and great ordeal.

"Baby, do you want to come? I don't think you should come. Do you want to come?" He rambles, "You can come. They will bring the body from Thessaloniki to his home. They will set him down in the room. All night everybody will cry and screaming and cry some more. It's not good. It's very bad. All night, no sleep, crying. I don't think you want it. You want to go? You can go. I don't think you should go. You can go. I don't think you want to go."

Usually my husband is so very direct with me, never mincing words, rarely repeating, nearly never unsure, no mixed meanings or double messages. So now I am confused, but I think I'm supposed to go, so I ask, "Am I supposed to go? Does Mama expect me to go? Is it all right not to go? I could stay here. I could... answer the phone."

Now that's a beauty. From Abbott and Costello to "Patricia's Advanced Greek Made Easy." Except for our immediate circle, who exactly is going to understand my broken Greek? And my voice. Now I speak enough like the rest so that the beginning of each of my sentences sounds fluid. Others will listen, understand and mistake me for Greek and will begin to speak loudly and quickly. I will apologize. I am the American wife. I speak very little.

But Kostas is convinced. "Yes Baby, this is good." He turns to his brother, "What's the number over there?" He replies "Threa, threa, enea, enea, pente." Now I know my first twenty numbers so although Kostas translates, I repeat with him and write down. "3-3-9-9-5. Bravo, Baby. Anybody calls give them that number. If they want Mama tell them she's at Leonidis' house. Tell them to call that number. Don't open the door. Tell anybody to go over there. Bravo, Baby, Bravo." He grabs and holds my forearms firmly, kisses me on the forehead then on the lips and says as sweetly as he can, "I see you later."

Okay. I have a job. Anatolios, I suppose not knowing what else to say, says, "Okay, Patricia, here's the fan. There's the air conditioner. Here is the phone. All is good? Yes," he answers for himself. "Here are Mama's keys if you need to go anywhere."

To which Kostas replies again in a manner against his character, "Don't go. If you need to go, you know where to go. Don't go though. Stay. Don't go. Don't open the door." With that they leave through the elevator, two brothers out on a mission.

I walk out to the balcony and watch them nervously walk down the street and around the corner. It's just 10 minutes past 7 pm.

I'm alone in a home where I'm never alone. It feels strange. I turn on the TV. Mama's soap opera "Lampsee" (Shining) is just beginning. For years I have watched it with her as she explains who's the brother and who's the sister and the father and which one is the good one and the bad one and the lover and the friend. Suddenly it doesn't matter anymore. I have no need to watch it. I know, I'll wash my hair.

So I go upstairs and take out fresh underclothes. The phone rings. It's Diana, an old friend of Leonidis and his first wife,

Aggie. "Yasoo Patricia," she says. I reply in Greek and she speeds into language. "Slow down", I say. "Remember, understand, take it easy. I have the number, the phone number." Yes, she has that too. But she wants to know what time the services are tomorrow. OOOhhh. Didn't think to get that information. So I direct her to call for it. I believe she thinks she should be there tonight and would prefer not to call, but I don't speak good Greek. "Okay then. I'll call over there. Thank you Patricia. You're a good girl. Bye, bye."

I love it. Everybody tells me I'm pretty. That I'm a good girl. A doll. They stare at me sometimes for too long. I feel like I'm ten years old at times. It's okay. I think it's the nice blonde hair and crystal blue eyes. In any case, it's nice to be admired. To be called a girl, a good girl, a doll and at 44. Yes, it's okay.

Since I took on the job of answering the phone, I'd better do it. So I pull out the extension cord and test the distance. I run the phone line first down the hall to the bathroom just outside the door.

Summertime water pressure is a big issue with Kostas and me at Mama's house. There isn't any, and the lack of it drives him absolutely crazy.

I turn the shower on. The head is attached and is supposed to hook on the wall but the joint is out of whack. So in order to keep it upright, I wrap the stem wire of a plastic flower around the handle. I wash and then put conditioner on my hair, soap my body and drip, drip, drip. "No way! No water. Oh poop."

The only alternate water sources are the kitchen or the hose upstairs. I opt for the hose, but I can't afford to get my only dark clothes wet by putting them on, and I'll have to pull that phone extension up the spiral stairs as far as it can go—that's 12 steps. So I wrap the towel as much around me as is possible, which is not much, and proceed in grabbing my clothes in one hand, the extension cord in my teeth, the phone and towel ends in the other and proceed upstairs. Thank God I'm home alone. It's a sight to behold, for sure.

Upstairs I change back into the loose fitting white shorts and blue sleeveless top, only this time without the benefit of bra and underwear. Out to the balcony where I proceed to rinse out my hair, bent over, with the hose. Just as the water begins to get clear, the buzzer buzzes downstairs. I pull over to the edge and look down the four flights. There's an old couple. "Parakalo," I scream. "Adara then einai etho." (Please... Adara (Mama) is not here.)

Buzzz, Buzzz, Buzzz. The old goober screams, "Open the door! We don't know you. We're here to see Adara! We have gifts for her." Buzz Buzz Buzz.

Here I am braless, still with soap on my body and conditioner in my hair, long thick hair, absolutely sopping, dripping wet and so too my clothes, as limited as they are. "Ena lepta. Ena lepta," I scream, which means "In a minute, in a minute." I shake my head like a dog to get rid of some of the water and run to the elevator.

Down to Mama's floor and out to her balcony. Buzz Buzzzz. I try again this time not so loudly from this, now the third floor. "Please. I am Patricia, the American. The woman of Kostas and my man told me no to the door."

Well, although I thought that was pretty good, it wasn't going to work with them. Perhaps they thought I was holding Mama hostage or something. Everyone knows she never leaves the house. In any case, the gruff buzzes again and again and hollers now very angrily, "Open the Door. What's the matter with you? We don't want you. We've come for Adara. Open the Door. Open I say."

That's it. I have the power. I was given it surely. I shout loud and firmly. "OHI, SIGNOMI, OHI." Which is "No, Sorry, No." They got the message because the old lady slips out into the street dodging a car or two as she looks up in desperation.

"Please," I interrupt her. "I'm sorry. My Mama Adara is within Leonidis home. Go. Adara is not here."

"Ohhhhh," she answers and limps over to the old buck. "Come on," she says to her terribly impatient hubby, "She's at Leonidis' house. Come on. Let's go." And as they turn away from the door the phone rings.

An officious sounding voice announces she's calling from Thessaloniki for "Adara Petras," pronouncing the last name as though she's not done it before.

"Sorry," I say. "I don't understand much, but I have the number."

Then the woman responds in English, that she seems genuinely proud to be able to use. "Oh, Okay. You speak English? Okay. And you have a different phone number? Okay?"

"Yes," I reply and continue to speak in Greek. "It is 3-3-9-9-5."

She repeats it back to me and then I confirm to which she replies, "Okay, Bravo. Very good. Have a good day."

I will, I think. At least now I have regained some confidence.

After watering Mama's plants, I sat down to a Swedish movie with Greek subtitles until Kostas came home at half past twelve. We went straight to bed.

At 5 am the cocks begin to crow across Katerini. The sun

hasn't quite risen but the rooster wakes up all the other morning birds. "I have to go," Kostas says as he sits up in bed.

"Baby, it's 5 am in the morning."

"I know," he says with resignation. "This is the way it is. I have to go back there. You go to sleep. I'll be back after 8 o'clock for some breakfast and I have to pick up my pants."

He refers to the tailor. He didn't come prepared for a funeral. He packed no dark pants let alone any serious slacks. We came to vacation. So shortly after his second visit to the hospital he stopped in town to have a pair of dark slacks made. They had called yesterday afternoon before we got the bad news. They were ready. And just in time.

Kostas had very appropriately made another stop yesterday after a visit with the estate lawyer. It was to the parlor. He had asked for prices and a guaranteed quote which I'm sure this business man had pre-negotiated. These fellows would pack the body from the Thessaloniki clinic. Prepare it for the wake along with presentation table and casket. Get it to the home, then to the church for services and then to the cemetery. I presumed the usual. And I have now learned that the official looking paper he held in his hands yesterday after getting the news, was the quote, the order from the parlor. He had called them to tell them it had happened.

So off he went, this man of mine. I tried to imagine, as he walked off, what they had been doing all night. And who were they. I knew it was Mama and it was at Leonidis' apartment so I guessed his wife would be there. Never mind for now, and I fell back to sleep.

I woke promptly at 7:15 and got out of bed. Unlike Kostas, I had very much anticipated possibly having to wear black. I had a black pullover and my dark brown/black patterned skirt. I'm glad it is calf length, as I didn't pack any stockings. I was a little chagrined at my newly pedicured feet, as all I had with me were sandals. I went with my conservative brown ones with the low heels, which also covered most of my feet.

Still, I thought I looked sufficiently and appropriately bleak and since only mourning Greeks, specifically widows, wore all black anyway, I was prepared. Brushed my teeth, rinsed my face and rubbed some Nivea around my eyes and on my forehead. I saved another five minutes by not having to apply mascara or lipstick. Instead of my usual perky braid to the side, I opted for a pulled back tight-to-the-middle style. And I was done.

The elevator did not open immediately on our floor. This was the cue that someone else had been in the house, as Kostas always takes the stairs. I pushed the button and prepared myself to see Mama. She wasn't there. Anatolios was, though.

He was in a light sleep in the middle room on the day bed. I reached over and slid the door closed. The clock said 7:25 am. Into the kitchen. I poured the juice, cut the cake and prepared the fruit on the tray. The phone rang. It was Dora and she asked to speak to Anatolios. I quietly told her he was asleep and I preferred not to wake him. Kostas should be here after 8 am, I let her know. "Okay. Thanks, Patricia."

I sat out on the balcony as the city began to wake to a new day. Dorcas had already taken his first delivery. He had had his bottling business across the street from the Petras family for over 35 years. Mama got all her bottled goods from him on account from Ouzo to beer, to orange juice, to Coca Cola. He is a stout man with a gray balding head. Much of the time he sits with others at a table in front of his business while his son and another move the cases about in his small warehouse. Right next to it he has a neat, well-kept storefront, with polished tile floors and a nice display window that I believe his daughter arranges and rearranges. In any case, the man is there, I now know, from 7am to 11pm with the exception of the standard 2 hour lunch break.

Two doors down is Noona. Noona means Godmother in Greek and that's just what she is to my husband. She's Mama's best friend from way back. Over the years she's gotten pretty much blind and it's difficult for her to cross the street, but she does it and more than occasionally. She has an ancient green cement house which appears to be in disrepair. It has a flat roof that holds the heat, and I've heard it's unbelievably hot in there in the summertime.

Still farther next to her, is a five story apartment house. On the third floor Vanora lives with her brother. She hollers at people with a sweet voice across the street and up and down. She was once an attractive young lady, I am told the most beautiful in Katerini. She's a year older than my husband and attended school with the boys. The story goes that she fell madly in love, head over heels, with a captain in the Navy. Though she was to be his bride and had her dowry all set, the cat got out of the bag. The captain was already married with two children of his own, no less. This betrayal broke her heart in two. Now all speak of how she was instead of what she is. There is sadness in her disposition, but sweet, very, very sweet.

On the other side of Dorcas is a four-story apartment building. There's a widow on the third floor who regularly entertains on her small balcony. She's sweeping it now as I write. In any case she nods at me when I water Mama's plants. I'm sure she can appreciate the diligence the job takes. Mama has commented on her kind ways. I appreciate that she has painted her floor a nice sienna color with darker trim and pretty roll up shades. A unique delight compared to most, which usually follow the same drab gray color.

Kostas won't be here for another twenty minutes or so and somehow reading People magazine doesn't seem appropriate. So counting on my fingers I begin to say the rosary. I'm surprised how well I have held on to the words of the Hail Mary and Our Father prayers. I feel pretty holy and begin to feel my spirit with God and possibly a good send off to my brother-in-law and his grieving family.

The phone rings and I jump up to answer. It's my husband, he's on his way. He'll buzz lightly then I'm to go downstairs and unlock the door. It's a little after 8, he's going to run by the tailor first, then come home. Have breakfast ready, he's hungry.

I put the water on for my coffee and prepare the ingredients for his frappé. Just ten minutes pass and the buzzer buzzes. I run to the elevator with Mama's keys in tow. I unlock the door. Kostas looks beat. "The tailor is not open. Alexis is coming. He'll be there at 11 to 12. I'm so tired and hungry." He refers to his younger brother, the singer who is flying in from Crete to Thessaloniki, then taking the bus to Katerini. Kostas seems to refresh a little knowing another brother will be there to share, and it's nice to have his abrupt speech back after last night. But whatever, he goes upstairs to freshen up. I let him know that Anatolios is asleep in the room and we should eat our breakfast down here in the case the phone rings. "Okay. No problem, but it's so God damned hot already." It's so true.

It's already plenty hot and it's not yet 9. It's going to be one of those hot, sticky humid Greek summer days and needless to say, it won't be a day at the beach.

We marked through breakfast with only a word or two. Kostas did mention that I wouldn't like it, that is, the funeral, but who would? After we finish he went upstairs to brush his teeth and then out to the tailor. While I'm cleaning the kitchen, Anatolios entered with the emptied glass. He thanked me for the orange juice I had set by his bed. He informs me that he will go home now to change into appropriate clothing. He will see us at the destination. He, too, looks terribly beat.

It's now a little after nine. Kostas brushes off my sweater and pulls at my waist. "Okay, let's go now." We kiss and head out the door.

We walk silently down the street. There is motion everywhere. The city is truly alive. For some reason I had believed that Leonidis' home was farther away from Mama's house than just past the corner and then a block down. As we approached the building, it was the top of the casket that caught my eye, leaning against the wall, a sign to all that a wake was within. The top half of the polished mahogany coffin had a large inlaid gold cross. Though it was standing upright, I note that the size is much smaller than ones in the states, and rather than rectangular it has six sides not unlike Dracula's tomb. My stomach quivers. As we walk in the hallway, I see six pedestal bouquets of deep dark purple mums, each with a sash and a brother's name on it. Kostas comments, "There are six here. One from each of the brothers and then one from Dionysius and Adarula, his son and daughter."

Adarula is Leonidis' grown married daughter. She lives in Athens with her husband, Yannis, who is a captain in the Marines. They have two children ages 9 and 11, and a new born just 3 month-old baby girl, whom her grandfather had never met. For now, or at least while she had visited her father in the hospital for the last two months, she has resided with her baby in their summer house in Litohoro village 10 miles from Katerini at the foothills of Mt. Olympus. The babysitter during her city visits was her mother's sister.

The voluminous house was originally built by Leonidis and his first wife on a lot that belonged to her parents which was split between her and her sister. It was to be their retirement home; unfortunately she passed away just before it was completed. Leonidis never really made it his own, and when he remarried, thought it appropriate to pass it on to their daughter and her family.

In any case, Kostas and I entered the elevator and pushed the button to the fourth floor. I was not prepared for what I was about to see. The elevator opens directly at the front door into the apartment. The door was wide open giving direct entry to the hallway, which is walled completely in beveled glass mirrors. Further on, there are more mirrored walls in the front room, which reflect the full contents of the living room, again a sight I was in no way prepared to see.

There in the middle of the room, set at table height is my dead brother-in-law, set in a shallow casket on a table with all furniture facing him. The body is perpendicular to me. On the far side, as though sitting at a dining table with her son before her, is Mama looking absolutely dreadful. Next to her is Adarula and then an empty chair next to her. On my side, facing away from me looking towards the casket, is Vangie. There's a couch at the foot with four ladies in black who I later recognize to be Mama's sister-in-law, Kostas' aunt, her daughter-in-law Catalin, her daughter Karina and another woman I do not know. Directly in front of me to the side are another three ladies on the love seat also facing Nidis.

There is a pitched moan of at least three women's cries at a time. More than half are rocking as they sob. I feel my stomach knot and I gasp out loud. Kostas orders me, "Take it easy, Baby." as he pushes me forward and slips out onto the veranda where I must presume all the men are.

I'm horrified and recall that the funeral is not until 12 pm or so. "Oh my God, I'm not going to sit here like them for three hours." Oh my God, I was so wrong.

I swallowed and concentrated on where I would best be positioned to console Mama if at all possible and at the same time be far enough away from the body to maintain sanity.

Adarula has come towards me. I reach out and give her an all body hug for some duration. She weeps and I hold and tickle the back of her neck and caress her face. In English she says, "Thank you. Thank you Patricia very much for coming. You're very kind." NO kidding I think, with no joke intended.

As I complete our embrace, I reach and bend over to give Vangie a kiss to the right and left and then I hear Mama's cry, "Patricia. Oh here you are. Look Patricia. Patricia. Here is my Leonidis. Look at him. Look at him. Here he is." Then she turns her conversation directly to him, touching his face. "Look Leonidis, my Leonidis, it is Patricia, come from America for you. Patricia has come. Look, Leonidis, it is Patricia."

I can't handle this. I just can't handle this.

Then the women's weeping gets louder. "Look Leonidis, it's Patricia, Leonidis."

I walk around the casket, trying not to give in. Mama takes my hand and moves it towards his face. Oh my God. I'm going to die. Oh, God help me.

He is that awful-looking dead color. His lips painted faint red. His mouth and nose have sores where the tubes were going in and out. His hair usually thick and full and nicely piled on the top of his head like all the other brothers, is slicked straight back showing the drawn and hollowed cheeks and face.

Instead of lying inside the coffin as is the means I'm familiar with, his face protrudes out, up and over the coffin which is just three inches away from the edge of his body. It's definitely a tight fit and he's right there, popping out, as though he's the turkey at the Thanksgiving Day table.

"Sit here, Patricia," says Mama as she pats the seat next to her. "Right here. There he is. Look at him. Leonidis, Patricia." I hug her but it's no use. She wants the three of us to communicate with each other. I bless myself and nod. Nonetheless Mama leans forward over her son and tells him, "Kostas and Patricia are here now, and Anatolios. We're all here."

Then into the room comes Dionysius. Poor sweet son. Can he possibly understand? His father is gone and all these crying women have been here since 6pm last night. He comes over and greets me. I hug him which confuses him because I never do that. But I give up my chair and now I am not in the front row seat.

Behind the three chairs is a step-up fireplace hearth, 4 feet on one side and 3 on the other. It's a near triangle, covered with carpet which looks soft and seemingly comfortable. I sit down behind Mama where I will remain until the 12 pm caravan to the church.

Mama starts to cry again, "My Leonidis, what do you want?" She asks, "What do you want my dear Son?"

Chara enters the room and begins a light scream at her brother-in-law. "Leonidis, look what you've done. Is this a good thing? No, it is not. Leonidis. Look what you've done!" She nods her head.

For the next 30 to 90 minutes there is a slow steady stream of folks coming in and out, and some hanging about. Most have brought flowers. Catalin immediately cuts the stems off and pokes the blooms into the empty, but quickly filling spaces about the body. He's beginning to look more tranquil now, in this bed of flowers and room full of weeping women.

At about half past 10 am, it begins to feel terribly cramped and hot in here. A trickle of sweat runs down my back. There is also the smell of sweet body odor in the room which gets dramatically stronger in volume and intensity as new and different mourners step up to condole.

A group of four women led by a stout leader arrive, proceed noticeably past Vangie, and go directly to Mama and Adarula. Once they are through with condolences, they scope out and survey my corner. The leader assigns seats, two on her side, the other two squished in next to me. She and her associate sit across from me, with no less than four and a half feet between our knees, which are all facing each other. Cute, cute, cute. Airflow comes to a virtual standstill as the intense smell of polyester and body odor, on twice-worn clothes without a wash, is vivid. Of course, the Greek custom of the ceremony taking place the very next day after death doesn't allow one to plan ahead and wash those mourning clothes.

Some stinkiness has to be expected, but really I feel like a chicken in an incubator. The women's shrill voices talking about everybody in the room and who they are and why they're not important is particularly catty, and I don't like catty. The old woman next to me has breath that could kill Mr. Ed. I am tempted to offer a mint, but after the going over I got when the big one, in the poked out at the big bosom poochy black blouse, discounted me as just Kostas' woman, I wasn't going to try and enter the "group." Then Big Mama Poochy gets up and in a loud boisterous voice shouts, lunges forward and points out towards the body, "You know who I am. I haven't gone anywhere. You'll see her. I'm here now and there you go Leonidis. There you go, and here I am."

There was absolutely nothing kind in either her disposition or statement to him. It was though she was the school yard bully letting him know that he wasn't going to get away from her by dying. Again she shouts, "You know me. You know who I am, Leonidis." She nods her head and looks at her group for confirmation and quickly scans the faces in the room as though we should all know.

Well, I didn't. And this corner was made no better by her presence. And she didn't smell good either. And sweat was pouring down her face and her hair was in dire need of style. I didn't like it. She was openly pooh, pooh to me and you can have her friends too. But this wasn't about us.

A short, fit man who I had seen and been introduced to in Nidis' carpet store on previous occasions stepped around the casket. He openly grieved and nearly collapsed with sadness as he walked around the body and gave Mama a hug. His sadness brought out the same in Mama and she began to chant and cry out to her son. The man scampered away out onto the balcony.

A broad-shouldered woman with a deep voice accompanied Noona to the body. It was clear that Noona couldn't focus properly, but she gave Mama a big hug and a warm kiss on the cheek. The occupants in the room continued to change positions. One of the ladies on the love seat, got up and gave Noona her seat.

Then Mama's sister Arissa came in with two younger men that I presumed to be her sons. She came around the casket, said some kind and gentle words to Nidis, kissed him surely and sat next to Mama who exalted, "Here's Aunt Arissa. Arissa, Aunt Arissa, Leonidis. Here's your Aunt Arissa."

Now the crowd and stream of mourners got steadily thicker. Some lingered. Some came and went. Some passed by the body altogether and stepped directly out to the balcony, which I later found houses nearly 25 tightly packed.

From time to time ladies who seemed to know me would nod or slightly wave the hand. The corridor hallway to the kitchen was full with some who were afraid, or just not properly prepared nor dressed to step up to the main circle. Vanora came in. She had on a French sailor type sweater that she had cinched rather tightly at the waist with a thick belt and a rather tight skirt. When she bent over her cleavage was apparent. It didn't bother me, I had seen her over the years bending and twisting before me on the balcony across the way. It was, however, evident the corner clutch didn't think her appropriate.

A woman of strong character with pretty, thick gray hair and striking eyes came around to kiss Mama. She looked over at me in full recognition and smiled graciously as she acknowledged who she was in Greek, which was completely

Greek to me. Another woman came by, who I recognized as the wife of the shoe store proprietor, a fellow schoolmate of Kostas, from whom we purchased shoes this, last and two years before.

And so it went on. At quarter of twelve, Alexis arrived. I hadn't noticed him in the crowd but was deeply stirred as was everyone else when he gasped and groaned and cried out loud. His legs gave way at the feet of his brother and he wept with abandon, so sadly, so hopelessly and helplessly. Now Mama had a new purpose. She rose from her seat and scuffled over to her fifth born son to comfort him. "It's okay Alexis, my love, my baby, my son. It's okay Alexis, Leonidis is with father now." Again she and her son Alexis wept and cried. Chara came over trying to offer support and none could be had. He was simply and surely inconsolable.

This new drama had set a new purpose. The carriers of the body had arrived. It was time to trek over to the church. Kostas had come in from outside and acknowledged his little brother's arrival, although he had not been there for the experience. He announced to me, "Baby, it's time to go. Don't watch these people move the body. It's not good. Go downstairs." Again he began to inquire whether or not I wanted to go home. "Honey Dear, I will go to the church. This is the right thing to do. Don't worry about me. You are family, Kostas. You make sure you do what you are supposed to do. Stay with the family."

"Yes." I was right and he nodded, glad for confirmation that he had some duty here. He furrowed his brow and nodded his head. He had a purpose in his sadness.

Like smoke once lingering and now drifting out of the room, the folks began to leave. Three by three they left by elevator and those strong enough filed down the four flights of stairs. I scuffled around the body and to the front door. By then the room was noticeably clear except for the immediate family and those worker bees humming around with their own silent purpose.

By the time I hit the second floor, the heat overtook me and I realized I had to slow down. I had been, after all, in dire want of air for 2 1/2 hours. Now was not the time to collapse.

The ground floor was very busy. We gaited out into the sun-drenched street. In a moment, the scalding temperature was evident. The light blinded my eyes. The sight was unbelievable. The road was a tight one with sidewalks on either side. The street was absolutely full to the brim with people all the way around the corner, to the front and to the back. The hearse was parked right in front and the family, who on foot would lead the procession behind it all the way to the church, would be the last to exit the building.

It was hot. It was really hot. Sweaty people were coming up to me, acknowledging that I was Kostas' wife and telling me who they were. Plenty just stared at me. Others pointed at me. I tried to just mingle into the crowd, but I was pushed forward, back up towards the hearse with the rest of the family.

Then out came Mama, accompanied by our cousin Karina, who had her arms about her. I watched to make certain she offered the proper support. Then out came Anatolios who nervously looked from right to left and squinted as he looked out into the crowd. He straightened his tie, repositioned his jacket and acted as though it wasn't too hot to be so fully dressed. Then he and the others made way as the carriers brought out Leonidis, who was still in open casket. They slipped him into the back and strapped in each side, then gathered the standing flower arrangements and propped and secured them to the top of the hearse. Although it didn't look so, all of this was done with precision and pretty quick timing. Within minutes the engine rumbled, a cloud of diesel smoke poofed out the back of the vehicle and off it went at a steady five miles per hour.

As if he had predicted that the exhaust would kill us, Kostas had snuck past and behind me into the crowd. He called, "Baby." I turned and pushed through the crowd to get to him. He didn't want to be in the first group, although he clearly belonged. They all made way for him. His manner of walking was different than it had ever been. He held both arms around behind his back and swayed a bit to each side as he stepped. I rested my hand on the bridge of his connected forearms.

It was just four short, albeit winding blocks to the church, this brother on a terrible mission that seemed to have no end, and it was hot, so terribly hot.

As we entered the driveway to the church I recognized it clearly. Kostas and I and Mama had been there many years before; it was the year of our marriage. We had sat before a council of six padres to request the acceptance of this Roman Catholic American girl and this once church-married and now divorced single man, and their marriage in this Holy Greek Orthodox Church. I remember the eight rose colored pillars. The fitted chiseled wood seats attached on all the walls of the church. The magnificent four domes of painted ceilings–scenes of Christ and the Madonna and Saints in marvelous combinations of color and depth. All the gold laminations. The pews in irregular shapes and different woods facing in varying directions but principally towards the altar. And now my eyes focused towards that group of four to five padres at the front of the church.

Leonidis had been placed before them, his head facing them. Mama and the other direct family were seated immediately to his left side. Purpled pummeled faces all in a row, Anatolios,

Vangie, Mama, Arissa, Adarula and Dionysius. Standing behind them were Anatolios' two grown children, brave soldiers weeping next to their mother, Chara. To the side and behind her were Kostas' cousins, Kostas and Catalin and Karina and her mother. The family all turned to us motioning Kostas towards them. I pushed him forward as much as he would go, but he didn't want to be too close to that front line.

The church has no ventilation whatsoever. A virtual sauna. Over two hundred and fifty souls and bodies gathered to breathe the air that was barely enough for two. And then the padres begin to chant. The incense begins to burn. The mourners begin to cry with new vigor. Beads of sweat accumulate from the back of my knees to the soles of my feet, the nape of my neck to the crease of my butt, between my toes, my breasts, under and across my brow and below my hairline, between and up and down my legs. It wasn't a roasting kind of hot, it was a steam bath, sauna type of hot. Really, really kind of hot. So in my mind I took myself away to where there is air. I flared my nostrils peacefully and drifted off. These were merely ghosts before me, faded and calm.

After the padres finished, a friend of Leonidis got up and read from the scriptures. And then his daughter got up. She's a strong, centered woman, mother of three. A good wife although like her mother, a bit overbearing and self righteous. She had her most recent child just three months ago yet was already in pretty good shape. She trembled at first, wary of the crowd and her responsibility but she gained her composure. Her statement was long and very personal. Perhaps it if had been in my own language and in a church at winter time I could have been more appreciative.

But for now it was a personal eulogy that brought suffering to a crowd of breathless hot sweaty people, who although all loved and cared deeply for the man she spoke of, needed nothing more than an oxygen bag and a cool glass of Sprite.

I continued to fan my husband. Folks were moving about a little here and there and the smell of sweet body odor of different sorts swelled over.

Then more incense and chanting and prayer and a short song. Soon an announcement was made that the family would leave first. They congregated at the back of the hall to accept condolences. Further, anyone who required a ride to the cemetery could get it in one of the two buses the family had provided and that would return to the church after the burial. I thought that curious, and later found it was an accommodation my husband had arranged.

And so the family, each him and herself, circled around the body, each kissing both him and the holy book that lay on his chest. Touching his face, saying goodbye. Kostas pushed me forward in front of the crowd already beginning to line up. I said goodbye to my brother-in-law, kissed my two forefingers and placed them gently on his forehead.

I noted now that Mama and Vangie and the rest of the family had already made their way to the rear in a seated row. I turned to Kostas and gently said, "Honey Dear, you have to be over there." He agreed and hustled into position. I found a seat nearby. Then one by one they walked by, holding, hugging, kissing and crying with the family. There was a bit of air coming from the front doors, which served well in moving around the body odors. It was evident that Kostas was clearly uncomfortable as one of the principal targets of all this kissing and hugging and carrying on with some familiar, and some not so familiar. All hot and sweaty mourners who just wanted to let him know how sorry they were. Soon enough the last had given their condolence and the casket was brought out the front of the church. There was a bit of a commotion figuring with whom and how the principals would ride over to the cemetery. The decision was made that Kostas and I would ride with George and George. As we hopped in the back of the Honda and took off, the second car behind the hearse, Kostas explained that Georgos was Arissa's son and therefore his first cousin. Georgos in the passenger seat had married Arissa's daughter. So these two, oh so looking and acting alike, nearly fifty, lightly balding Georges were brothers-in-law.

Our conversation on the way to the cemetery consisted mostly about cigarettes. George, the driver, was congratulated for having just stopped smoking 8 months ago after smoking for some 35 years. Kostas had told them of his lung cancer surgery back in '83 that had, praise the Lord, successfully saved his life, and also rid him of the terrible habit. The other George lit up a cigarette just as we arrived, the first moment out of the vehicle.

We managed a well-placed parking spot in the front of the gates. Behind us the 2 caravanning buses stopped and the folks all filed out. The car that brought Mama and Arissa, and Anatolios' sedan which carried most of the other principals, drove through the gates right up to the site, just behind the hearse.

I had been here many times before. My husband had made it a habit to visit his father's grave at least once each year. On these occasions, I saw a very solemn serious side of him come out, as he quietly showed his respect.

This cemetery consists entirely of above-ground marble box graves, unlike the ones I have known in America, which are principally underground. The headstones show that often husbands and wives and sometimes children are buried therein together. There are photographs showing a picture of the entombed on each box. Each row marked with numbers, with nearly 50 per row to the left and just 15 to the right of the driveway. We were headed for row 37, about 10 from the right. I noticed that father's marble box had been broken through and partly removed to make room for his son who would be buried upon him.

The ground was already open and as the burying team brought up the casket, Kostas asked me not to watch. The box was lifted via stretcher-like tape bands and lowered directly into the soil. As mother and daughter filled their shovels and began to lightly bury the body, we heard Mama's deep sad cries, "My Leonidis, my dear boy, my sweet Nidis."

And now his daughter moans, holding her heart, "Father, my father."

And then all other cries whistled through the yard just as loud, just as sure. They began a walk around the grave, a ritual whereby one of the caretakers holds up a shovel full of dirt and the folks stand in line to throw a pinch down and say their final goodbyes.

Kostas told me to go and do it but it was something in which I preferred not to participate. Then the six huge purple flower arrangements were laid one on top of the other, on top of the grave. The two main priests from the church came forward to the site and began their chanting prayers. The weeping got still sadder and louder and the incense burned and folks lit candles and stuck them right in the dirt and in a little altar box next to the grave.

I stood nearby watching as Mama bent over her son's grave crying to him until she was hoarse. As the ground was uneven, I had make certain she was on firm ground. I came behind her and pulled her arm gently forward to which she surprisingly obeyed.

By then Kostas called to me from the stairs to the left of the gravesite chapel. "Come here Baby. In here. Bring Mama. I'm saving your seats here. Come on, Baby." What could he possibly mean? Now what? Then as I followed the buzzing crowd I noted there was a small hall with rows of long set tables.

Each place had a little offering plate of sweet bread, a cookie, two dark olive looking ovals, some feta cheese and a shot of liquor. The folks had all gathered around for this mini feast. They seemed genuinely excited and pleased about the refreshment laid before them. After getting Mama seated next to Anatolios I sat down myself and put what I thought was an olive in my mouth. It turns out it was a chocolate covered, malt like nut candy. It took me by surprise, but it was yummy.

Kostas had left me behind. I reached over and took my second glass of brandy and in two quivering gulps it was gone. It was warm in my throat. For the first time I felt a sort of relief; my body felt a little cool and refreshed, as I was hot-breathed and a little high.

Lukas Will Have It

The husband is so affectionate. He's quick to compliment a woman who crosses over into our world and if she be among our most intimate circle, well, she can expect to be made to feel extra special, really attractive and yes, very sexy. I've watched him work my own sisters and sisters-in-law many a time.

But such cannot be the same in my case. I am expected to keep a hands-off, no kissy, huggy, feely regard for those of the opposite sex, relation or no. Yes, if it's been a while, a European kiss, kiss, to the right and left cheek is appropriate enough, at least from the in-laws, but cross over and the green-eyed monster will seek his wrath.

In the case of six brothers, it can sometimes get difficult. Take for example his brother Dionysius. Kostas has been and continues to be extremely affectionate with both the current and ex-wives. Full on hugs, and kisses and caresses given to make them feel feminine. I have never felt uncomfortable.

He's a good brother and blood is blood. I, on the other hand, have felt the full brunt of recourse from Dionysius in the way of expressed hurt feelings, declaring me cold and aloof when I've failed to reciprocate honest but intimate brother and sister-in-law exchange. I simply prefer that to the alternative which could very well lead to marital discord. Who needs that?

Lukas, Kostas' brother and fourth from the top, lives in Washington State with his wife, Susan. They have two grown sons who, when younger, lived some time in Greece. Right now, Lukas and Susan have another home in progress in Katerini, Greece just about 10 kilometers from Mama's. This interesting spacious home was designed by Lukas and has been under construction, I would say, for about 15 years.

Lukas and his brother Dionysius came to my office with their cousin not four months ago. Lukas came in, having not seen me for a couple of years, and declared I looked just fantastic. He did not settle nor intend to settle for the kiss kiss cheek cheek and, in fact, hugged me, pulling me into him, so much so that I had to push my palms against his chest to stop the chest-to-chest contact which had already commenced. Now, granted we hadn't seen each other in a long while, but had my dearest been present, I would have been asked what was all that about? I can only speak for myself, it means nothing to me.

Anatolios, the second brother from the top, and I have a loving relationship that rarely involves bodily contact but nonetheless is pretty special. He's the closest to Mama and so when we visit, a great deal of time is spent in cross company. He appreciates not only the love and care I show towards his mother, but certainly he must respect my ability to keep his brother enthusiastically involved for 22 years now.

We gave each other a peck of affection at the airport pickup but most time was devoted to the brothers' reunion and I just admired the love. I serve him cut fruit when making our breakfast, and ask him every time he's present downstairs at Mama's whether he'd like a cold Coca Cola or iced drink. Whether or not he accepts it, he always expresses his gratitude.

I am a totally giving person, no doubt. I honestly get pleasure from bringing it to others. It's who I am and everyone who I care anything about can see it, if not experience it first hand. For example, four nights ago we went out to the village town of Kitros for dinner.

There were seven of us and just as many bottles on the table; some beer, wine, water, Coke and Sprite. I've observed over time my nephew Thanos loves Coca Cola. I've never commented on it. At dinner I noticed the bottle of Coke at his end of the table was empty and there stood a full bottle way over at the other end of the table. I reached for it and gave it to him. At 24 years of age, I saw him chuckle as though he were 10 years old all over again, yet give me a man's nod for being so observant and caring.

Back to Brother Lukas. When we arrived at the Thessaloniki airport Anatolios alone was there to greet us. By the time we got over to the rental car station he had dialed his brother Lukas on the phone, handing it to me. After a combined 20 hour transit, a simple, "Hi, how are you?" is all I could muster. After all, we would be seeing each other soon and often enough shortly. Both Kostas and I were very brief in our salutations.

Since our 50 minute auto travel time to Katerini was spent in two cars, that is Anatolios in his and Kostas and I in our rental car, the two brothers had little time to catch up. So when we reached the lot next to Mama's house I elected to grab our two carry-ons and head straight to the house while the brothers stayed behind to chat. I rang the buzzer and it was Lukas who answered the intercom, "Nei?"

"Eimai Patricia," I said in my usual reply. "I am Patricia."

"Ella, Ella Patricia," Lukas responded, continuing to press the loud buzzer until the door was open.

I climbed the 10 steps to the elevator and up to Mama's floor. As I walked in, Lukas hurried to me with open arms and kisses of hello. “How are you, my beautiful sister-in-law?”

“I’m fine, the boys are downstairs.” He didn’t seem to appreciate that reply as I went to the kitchen to catch a cold drink.

As I got in there I was shocked and dismayed to see that Mama had no doors on her cabinets.

“Ti eina?” I asked.

“Oh,” he answered with a happy tone, “I’m refinishing Mama’s cabinets.”

My hand flew to my heart as I recalled that he’s been working on his own house project for some fifteen years without completion.

“Oh Lukas,” I gasped, looking under the sink and below the pull-out kitchen drawer that displayed a Tupperware catastrophe in one, slopping olive oil, bottles and cans and other messy stuffs under the other.

“Monon tris meras, you hear me Lukas, monon tris meras.” Only three days I so ordered him, only three days.

Then Mama came in through the hallway and gave into tears on seeing me. Lukas shrugged and went to greet his brother and help with the luggage. He was none too pleased with me.

The feeling was mutual.

Later that evening before leaving he came over and hugged and kissed me again. I noted Kostas acknowledging his action, but without comment.

It was two full days before Lukas and I saw each other again. Kostas and I had arrived home from the afternoon at the beach, making it our fourth swim event so far. My hair was messy and I was salty and hardly felt attractive. Anatolios and Mama remained seated. Lukas, however got up immediately and hugged me and exclaimed, "Oh my beautiful Greek goddess. You look so beautiful."

"How 'bout the cabinets? Tris meras, remember?" I answered.

Then he grumbled about what work he and his laborers had been doing while we were "on vacation." The boys visited awhile and then again, before I left to go upstairs, he got up and hugged me.

Shoot. I needed Kostas' help. I knew he didn't like his brother or anybody kissing and hugging me so I told him, "I don't know what's up with your brother, but you should let him know if the hugging thing is bothering you."

"NO." he replied. "That's your job. Tell him. Tell him you don't like it."

"But it doesn't bother me. I know it bothers you, so tell him."

"NO." he replied again. "It's your job."

Just two days later, we came home from our afternoon Leptokaria trip and much to my surprise, Lukas came through the entry and guess what? He had the cabinet doors. As he installed them, I warmed my string bean vasoolaki dish with meatballs, made him a salad and cut him fresh bread and watermelon. Set the table as I would for my own husband.

"My goodness, Patricia," he said as he sat and ate like a king, "This is so wonderful. Perfect. My favorite. You are the most amazing, beautiful girl in the whole wide world." I nodded and slipped upstairs to avoid an anticipated hug and kiss.

The next day after we came home from the beach I noted a big man's slice taken out of the macaroni dish I had made in the morning prior to trekking to the beach. Mama had given some to Lukas. And the day after that I got up early before our morning beach run to make my superb Chicken Bay, which is Mama's recipe. I also noted before we took our trek that Mama, with Anatolios looking on, was scooping out a good portion into a Tupperware that he was going to take to Lukas.

That night he gave me a big hug. I told him to stop showing so much affection, it made Kostas uncomfortable. "But it makes me so warm and comfortable," he replied. Kostas and

I tangled that evening about it.

The next day, Lukas came over and exclaimed how he adored my cooking, and especially that rice dish. "Rice?" I asked. "You mean the macaroni?" As Kostas found the dish disturbing, I said "Oh, let me warm up a plate for you."

"Oh, would you?" and came forward to me.

"Let me give you a big hug and kiss."

I stopped him and said firmly, in Greek, in front of Mama, "You have to stop. Kostas doesn't like it and I don't want you to hug me every time you see me."

He went on, "But you're so wonderful."

I interrupted. "Lukas, Parakalo. Stop. I mean it."

He looked bewildered. He went to hug me after eating. I snapped at him again, which he ignored.

Off and on the struggle continued, letting up only by me leaving the room. Then a few days before he left for home, he asked, "And how is my darling sweetheart Greek goddess today?"

"What are you thick?" I said in the meanest voice I can muster.

"What's that my blonde Greek beauty?"

"Will you stop, please."

"Why, I call Susan 'honey' all the time, and she's hardly that."

"She's your wife."

"And you're my beautiful sister-in-law."

"And you're a complete potato head, and I mean it."

I went upstairs.

The day he left for Athens, we gave each other a platonic farewell. And yet I am almost certain he has forgotten it all by now and we'll have to go through this again.

I'm so sweet honeybees swarm around my mouth. Geez.

Big Man, My Office

Late last week, we had trekked away from our regular beach sites on past the ancient village of Litohoro. We headed southbound, down the highway about 20 kilometers from Katerini and on one of the many bases of Mount Olympus. Just before Platamonas, we found Leptokaria, or did it find us? In any case, it's our new afternoon routine.

Leptokaria is a great little beach town, or rather village, with a row of sweet comfortable hotels along the main road that runs parallel to the sea. Nice little cozy restaurants with seaside coffee shops and quaint lodgings all through the village. The water is surprisingly chilly, especially salty, deep and full of currents. The sun sets later in the day making the day longer.

We've arrived back home Thursday evening, shortly after 9 pm. It's still light and humid, but certainly not half as warm as it's been for many nights before.

We let ourselves in the bottom door and start our escalade up the first flight of stairs when we hear Anatolios with Mama in the background calling out, "PAAAATRICIIIA, Ella, Ella, einai to mitera sou. Le telefono. Ella, Ella."

"Come. Come, it is your mother on the telephone. Come. Come."

Yikes. I thought we were completely incognito. It immediately occurs to me that my mother does not have the phone number here in Katerini so how and why could she be calling. Could something be the matter? Hmmmm. I had called the states and spoken with her Sunday, but it was I that called and I did not give the phone number to her, nor did she ask for it.

I pondered for a moment as I scaled the steps, how could she get the number? The only way to get it would be to go through last year's phone bills, when a couple of calls were made from the states while we were away on our last trip.

Oh no. So it has got to be an emergency of some sort. Even though it was oh so hot, I sped up the stairs as quickly as I could.

There in the living room sitting side-by-side, are Anatolios and Mama, the two who have the least command of the English language in the entire family. In fact, they have none. There's a lot of sign language, hand gesturing and face making going on.

Patricia's mother calling all the way from America and at the very same time, the latch of the door downstairs clicks. Marvelous timing! Clap hands! Goody, goody, joyous. Together, they seem so very pleased or at the very least, relieved that our timing was so good.

Though they were pleased, they were wide eyed with wonderment. What could possibly be the matter? Could there be some sort of urgent or special circumstance causing Patricia's mother to call all the way from America?

"Nei?" I answer the phone, which is Greek for yes.

It's my Mom and as usual, she's in tune.

"Nothing's the matter," she says, and continues. "Kiss Mama for me, say hello, Tell her right now everything's okay. Go on." she says, or rather orders me. "Do it. Everything is okay."

I love hearing her voice, but as always she's concerned with what Mama and Anatolios might be worried about.

"Allos entaxie." I say to Mama, repeating it, looking at Anatolios then back at Mama, "Se Agapo."

"All is okay. 'I love you,' she says to you, Mama," I tell her.

Back to what might be a matter of great urgency.

"So what's going on, Mom?"

She doesn't stumble on words or sentiment. "It's Mike Munson," she says strongly.

"What about him?" I ask in my own particular bothered manner.

After all, I worked like a son of a gun for three long months. I need three full weeks to get away from it all.

Mom bears down even though she knows I really don't want to be thinking about business and continues, "It's just an extension. He needs a copy of it for something…"

She continued with the details and we discussed procedure and yes, of course I agreed that he was important enough to have called me. But more important, how did she get the number? After we chuckled like Mommy and Patty, I politely asked, "So, how did you get the number? I'm afraid I didn't leave it for you."

"Well," she said pausing and getting comfortable, "I called Jo. And we came together into the office. That would be yesterday. You know I still can't drive." We both pause.

Then she says with irony in her voice, "But strange enough, you've made her in charge of your office and yet Jo doesn't have the phone number where you can be reached."

I sigh out loud for such a (purposeful) omission as she continues, "So I called everybody I could think of—Margo, Cathy, Kathleen, Ceal. Nobody had the number. I started to panic.

"Then you know, your sister Kathleen, she steps in and she says 'Let me see what I can do.'" Mom imitated Kathleen's clever tone.

Mom continues, "So she called me back an hour or so later. She had called the Carpet Store in San Francisco and nobody there could help. One of the salespersons told her maybe she could call Thanos, Kostas' nephew, at the warehouse. I want you to know, Patricia, and let Kostas know that Thanos was very, very careful, reluctant. Kathleen said she had to pull out some stops and pitches to make him give her the phone number. Kostas should know how protective his nephew, Thanos, was of the phone number. But Kathleen did it. She called me back with it," she said in a state of accomplishment.

"Of course, by then it was too late to call, or early. What time is it?"

"After 9 pm now, Mom." I replied.

We chattered some more and agreed that among other things, Mike Munson owed me some flowers to be delivered around the 16th when I was to return. Hah, Hah.

Then we finished up and said our goodbyes and I love yous, I miss yous.

I'm quite relieved and pleased as I got off the phone. But before I have time to reflect on the wonders of my own Mommy, there before me sit the two Greeks, Mama and Anatolios looking up with question marks reflected in their eyes and that same attitude in their bodies.

I went over and kissed Mama and told her. "Mitera mou milea Se Agapo kai theli ena fili."

(My Mom says I love you and give you a kiss.)

As I look at the two of them, it is evident that they know full well that that was not the reason my mother called all the way to Greece. They sat and eagerly awaited facts and reasons.

I could make it up, or I could tell the truth which frankly, really wasn't that exciting a story. But it is difficult to jump into full Greek right after speaking so kindly and lengthy with my own mother, in my own first language, so I opt for the short sweet truth.

Putting the tip of my index between my two eyes I mimic the act of translation.

"Hhmmmmmm." I ponder out loud as I make my short entry and exit into and then out of Greek, and then say boldly and without question or lack of authority, "Migalo Andre, to Graphio Mou."

"OOOHhhhh." They both nodded with understanding that Patricia was a business woman. "Neiiii." They agreed that she was so much more.

I chuckled and laughed out loud as I walked up the stairs. I'm so very smart in my office, a virtual big shot. I have my hands in and know just about everything I care to, and here, here in Greece where I come every year, I lack the skill to communicate such a simple concept and am reduced to describing it all in four simple words, "BIG MAN, MY OFFICE."

A Washing Machine

Disobeying all rules of grammar and punctuation, misdirecting, using or misusing vocabulary into double and triple meanings, innuendo, pokes, metaphors, similes and homilies, I nonetheless have what I consider to be a respectable, if not downright profound command of the English language.

This is exactly what makes it so impossible, so mind-bendingly frustrating when I am forced into a deadly mix of anger and the inability to properly verbalize. So very often I must stop, hold myself still and give it the what-for under my breath. If I could only say it in Greek…but then it wouldn't take so many words to tell.

Trust me, no one more than I would like Mama's washing machine to work correctly. Before I started the sardines, I opened her machine and saw and smelled a couple of mildewing pieces therein. It wasn't so deadly, so I set the wash, added the soap and some bleach, and left them be. Remember? I called Kostas to the balcony for a private consult while you all were waiting for me to serve cold drinks and the fresh sardines. I was overjoyed. The machine seemed to be working just fine and I just had to let him know about it. After another hour and ten minutes or so after starting, I had put my head in the machine and found that the wash was fresh-smelling, if not particularly white and clean. So I went upstairs and gathered two dresses and a good part of the first week's worth of dirty laundry. And did it all again, minus the bleach. After yet another hour and ten minutes, and well after all of you had devoured the sardines and watermelon, I again took a plastic bowl to the machine to take out the wash.

Now what's this? Oh my word, the clothes are sopping wet. So now, it's three bowls worth, heavy to say the least, that I must take upstairs to hang.

First, of course, each item requires a good and thorough wringing before clipping to the line. I shared my sadness at the continuing dysfunction of the ancient washing machine with its owner's third son when he came upstairs to the balcony. My worries at the beach today had been quite real. I was painstakingly reminded that it was happening all over again.

Just like last year when my frustration with the ailing machine had me hand washing linens and clothes in addition to the wringing, because Mama kept saying the machine worked just fine, and Kostas didn't think the last two weeks' worth was truly worth ruining the vacation with the familial uproar a denial of his mother's word might cause. And a member of this upstanding, oh so important family of the community be caught at the mat? And certainly the low-level village people at the cleaners to perhaps view a possible spot of misbegotten ejaculate on his underwear? No. Me, I remain, a washing machine.

Because it's been raining, there was no reason to talk or think about washing clothes. There's no dryer in this residence and where would I hang wet clothes? But as the sky began to permanently clear today, I applied thoughtful regard to the first week of dirty laundry. At the beach this afternoon, I told Kostas that I was nervous about the machine, and what was his reply?

"Ahhh stop it, Baby. This is so great. You're being negative. Try it. If it doesn't work, we'll just buy a new one."

Well, I certainly agreed with him. But there is something about replacing things in an old person's home-removing something with which they have grown familiar. They are comfortable enough so as to have forgiven its slight or even gross digression from the proper delivery of true purpose. Especially, for goodness sakes, when it's your mother-in-law and her home. And don't forget Patty dear, you have to inform this same fact to Mama's eldest living boy, who is knocking at the 70-year old door; who himself thrives on change as much as she. Hah.

And so as I go about wringing and hanging, I start my private preliminary conversation with myself….the argument that calls for replacement.

My husband has been using the same two towels for a week. Do you think he does that at home? Never mind that Mama has an extra drawer or two of what you might consider to be clean towels and bedding, just look at the one she's currently using as a blanket these days when she curls up on the couch. Is it not filthy? And that little shoulder blanket she's got around her when you jack up the air conditioners, would you put that on your newborn? Just how am I to ask? Don't you think the matriarch of this particular family would have these things clean and crisp if she weren't 90 and if it were just as easy as throwing them in the wash? When did you put the help on leave anyway? I could be at a fancy hotel; instead I'm really here to help. Naw. Ah poop, I am just a trouble-making in-law, right? So after the job, I grudgingly come downstairs to find the brothers yelling at each other. "Baby," Kostas hollers as I walk in, "Anatolios says the washer works."

"Yes dear" I humbly reply, "It does work but the spin cycle, it needs fixing."

He answers, "Very well, we'll just buy a new one." All the while brother Anatolios is in the kitchen wash closet, pushing and turning the knobs, each and all of them. Lights are flashing and the water's switching on and off and he's yelling, of course in Greek, over the sounds, "See, it's working. No problem. Come here, Patricia. Look, listen."

I try, God all mighty, I try to ignore the worthless passion and bear down to the solution.

"No Kostas, we don't necessarily need a new one. We need a repairman. It's just the spin cycle."

He answers, "Anatolios says the guy has been here twice and that it's fixed."

In the background, Anatolios is still the madman at the controls. "Listen, look, see Patricia, look, the lights, the water, it's definitely working just fine."

Ding, dong, ding.

It takes a while but this brain works well and it all finally clicks. This man has not used a washing machine in his lifetime. He wouldn't know where the soap goes. Certainly he doesn't know what the spin cycle is. Come to think of it, Mama has had this particular Greek machine since I've been in the picture. What's that, 23 years? Can cycles even be segregated on these old geezers?

Now Anatolios is screaming again at Kostas, and Kostas back at the brother. Here's another man who has no fricking idea what a spin cycle is. Like, "what's a Downey, dear?" And I think, oh gosh, who exactly is going to or has been explaining the problem to the repairman anyway?

Me, hah, I think not. I'd just be pantomiming wringing towels or the machine going round and round. Mama, who certainly doesn't want to part with her silly old machine, who probably will tell him it works just fine the way it is? Anatolios, Kostas? Please, stop pushing buttons. Get serious already. And so the decision is made, at least in my mind's eye. We will get a new one. But for now, the drama continues.

Oh, my dear brother-in-law has now advised his brother, and he is passing it on to me, that Patricia doesn't know how to use a washing machine. Hmmmm. Please don't poke me with a knife unless you're prepared to defend yourself on the rebound, dear Anatolios. I flinch, not intending to wound as much as get a new machine.

"No problem, dear," I respond. "You asked that I wash the jeans you have on. Go ahead take them off, let's try it."

"I'm not taking my pants off," answers he.

"Well, I've got a partial load upstairs. I'll bring it down. Anatolios can show me and make sure I really know how."

Kostas sees the logic, bites the bait and repeats it; I'm sure adding his own particular emphasis. He certainly intends to withdraw from the battle, the line of fire and happily hand Anatolios the weapon.

Holy shit, all hell breaks loose and like any man (or woman for that matter) who has lost the war and the battle too, Anatolios starts shaking and screaming at the top of his lungs as though this silly and ridiculous behavior might somehow checkmate my king.

Now, I must make amends; wave the white flag as it were, before I go for the kill without bloodshed, and use every womanly, sisterly technique.

"Signome, parakalo signome althelfos mou," (Sorry, please I'm sorry my brother.) I plead in the sweetest voice I can muster.

"Katalava, parakalo. To andre, to iatro, to pethi, to althelfos mou. Eyo monon thelo katharo ta rooha mou. Monon. Afto einai. Parakalo kei Ef faristo." (Understand please, the man, the doctor, the son, my brother. I only want to wash my clothes. Only, that's it. Please and thank you.) And for a little drama I throw in a handful of tears, lift and lower my arms in plea, then in resignation I bow my head, shrug, turn and walk away.

Snickering to myself, of course, but still wondering, could that have done the trick? It's Greek to me.

In the meantime, my dresses and towels and panties are flapping in the evening air. It's a quarter to 11 when I've finished writing and go in for a shower, as the boys are out for their evening romp.

It's a quarter past midnight, a little over twenty-four hours later, and the swish-swish of the new Siemens washing machine is on its second load. The three of us (the Siemens, Mama, who sits beside me hoping for a chat, and me) are keeping good company.

No checkmate, indeed. No need to paste my mustache.

You see, last night when he came home, Kostas had advised that we wouldn't be going to the beach until after noon. He, Anatolios and Chara (the doctor's wife) were going to rendezvous and head to the appliance store around the corner and buy a washing machine. The prescribed time: 11:30. The prerequisite: a machine in stock and delivered, and the old one taken away the same day, or no deal. Kostas was back home by one and we beached in Katerini for an hour or so and another three at Leptokaria.

On our ride home, having never eaten lunch, we spoke of the meal he wanted when we got home and how he was going to have it on the balcony upstairs.

"Warm the mousaka that Chara made, make one nice full salad, carpoozy and feta and I believe we have some of those sardines left over from last night. And beer, yes, I want beer."

As we arrived, Anatolios and Mama sat on the couch and chair keeping company, seemingly waiting for us (or at least his brother, her son). Kostas stopped and joined them.

I swooshed the damp towels and swimming suits up the elevator, hosed and hung them on the line and shuffled back down to Mama's floor, to the kitchen. I asked my brother-in-law if he would like some ice cream. Oooooh, yes. He smiled with delight and clapped his hands like a child, his thanks that there were no longstanding stonewalls between us showing in his eyes.

Still in the kitchen, I started dinner. Kostas was in the shower and the casserole was all warmed up by the time the salad fixings were fixed. But before I cut the fresh bread the buzzer rang. As Anatolios got up to answer it, I opened the sliding door and hung my head off Mama's balcony looking the two floors down to the front door.

Tah-Dah! A washing machine! It was he, the delivery man.

Oh, my. I got the salad, melon and cheese, bread, mousaka, napkins and utensils on the tray and zoomed up the steps, leaving the tray on the side table just up top the stairs. Ran back down, took off my apron, took out a table cloth, two mugs, bottle of beer, bottle of water and was on my way back up when I heard men's voices in the stairwell. Ah, just in the knick of time.

I let Kostas put the cushions on the chairs while I set the table.

It was quite charming, really; romantic, perhaps, except for the dog barking at us from the balcony just across the street. I wasn't sure whether he was barking at anything or anybody or whether it was just that we looked so unfamiliar in our comfy setting. Kostas screamed back at him, to no avail. We took it easy though and enjoyed ourselves until at the end I got up to clear the table.

"No. Sit back down," he ordered. "Leave them alone. They will cry at each other for a while." (Referring to the mother and other son.) "And when they are through, then it will quiet and then you can go and see."

We chatted and kept company for another 10 minutes or so and then Anatolios called up to me, "Patricia, come here. Let the man show you what to do."

So I hustle the tray and myself downstairs. Anatolios is

nervously pacing the living room and points to the kitchen.

Now the wash room, or wash closet, as it were, is in the itty-bitty walk space between the kitchen and dining room. There are two small doors, side by side. Both must be opened to get at the machine, but when opened do not allow for passage from either direction. The width between the open doors is less than three feet and there is less than two feet from the front of the machine to the back of the wall.

I can see from their backs that both Mama and the installation man are nestled between the two opened doors. The man is trying to explain it to her as patiently as he can. Mama is asking questions; he is repeating over and over.

I peek my head around the doors. Now this is something else. Mind you, at 7pm it's got to be 90 degrees and in the kitchen five more. Mama has a spotlight propped up on a little shelf not a foot from this young fellow's head. He has a very thick head of hair and sweat is pouring from his temples. She continues comparing its functions to the old machine and Anatolios is behind me, now jabbing in his own remarks.

I open the freezer and take out some ice and plop it in a tall glass of Coca Cola and hand it around the corner. All the while Mama is looking perplexed and the young fellow continues to perspire, leaning one arm on the machine; his body is just inches from her face. He looks at me as though I have thrown him a lifesaver. Mama has had enough already. She closes the door on her side and shuffles out of the kitchen. I try to take her place but realize I'm just too buxom. There's no way the two of us could be in that small space without bumping soft spots. So I hold the door half open with my neck around it.

"I have only one question," I say in my limited Greek. "Do you have a book in English?"

He shrugs, giving a look of total defeat, but after all I did give him that cold drink and had dismissed mother.

"I know a little English," he replies in equally broken English. "What do you want to know?"

Hah. That's it. Beautiful, I thought.

"How 'bout the whole trouble-shooting section?"

Of course, we won't need that until something happens. He walks me through the main stuff and we agree that the store just might have the book in English.

"I will check tomorrow."

So now it's quarter to one and Kostas has just shouted down the stairs, "Baby, are we going to go to bed tonight?

"Yes, dear," I whisper getting up to the staircase. "Just as soon as this wash is through." And to my relief, I do believe that's the spin cycle on a washing machine I hear.

Summer Bondage

Waking up late, leaving for the Katerini beach in town for the morning. The tide at this rich and sandy yet smooth beach declines slowly into the sea allowing for play of all sorts with your feet always touching the ground. I like hand standing with my feet perpendicular at the water's top, kicking my feet like a child. Or water aerobics at the chest level 20 yards out. Or floating on my back with my boobies as buoys atop me. Or when at its smoothest, just backstroke, breaststroke or crawl; or swimming laps without boundaries. The water's so warm close to the surface, almost bath like. Unlike Leptokaria.

So after a cappuccino here, three swims and lazing around with an icy strawberry granita in between. Simply divine, until about 3. Then another source and thick slice of pleasure.

We pack up for the beach below Mount Olympus where the snow melts into the sea making it brisk and tingly.

This is the beach of Leptokaria. No slow decline here. Smooth but rocky beach floor goes out just eight or nine feet and the water delves deep, deep deeper so that just 15 feet out the sea is as many more below me.

And when the Aegean speaks at this shore below the land of the Gods, the waves are known to crackle and swell and overcome. And the crazy tax lady, after curving her feet and toes over the big round pebbles has unbridled herself into the moving liquid, and with it, becomes so herself. If one were close enough to hear her most common sing song sung is the melody of Flipper. Flipper, flipper, flipper…

And she is most definitely and dynamically a dolphin. Cracking the waves, diving into and out of them. Kicking up her feet, legs, breasts, buttocks. Swishing in and out and atop and below. The salt is strong. Her face is reddened by the sun and the hours of swimming with her hair burning more golden in the sun and the sea, with just short breaks, that is until about 7 pm.

Trek the 15 kilometers back home. Shower. Moisturize.

And so I sit here next to Mama once again. Keeping company? No, not really. She lies on the settee next to me whilst I'm here with my tan feet on the coffee table reading. A thick book it is, and she's acknowledged as much with her eyes and actions. She has a very difficult time understanding why such a fun loving little ole gal like me could spend so much of her summer reading books.

Okay, it's 600 some odd pages. My second one of such thickness so far these first 10 days of my vacation and she knows I find this one particularly engrossing. And what is it that I read? Somerset Maugham, *Of Human Bondage*.

Now think, should you know the story. You are about to tell what it is about in a very limited manner, but hopefully convey more than the gist and why you would be particularly possessed.

Like most non-readers, she doesn't understand the reader's purpose, or involvement. It's as though instead of really being involved, you're simply waiting for something more interesting to occur, like, possibly human companionship. Hmmmm.

And so she asks. Realize that my Greek is broken and it her only language. "What are you reading, what's it all about?"

Okay, here goes.

"There's a boy, nearly a young man. His father died when he was just six and his mother passed away when he was nine. He went to live with strict padre (church) and his wife. He has a club foot."

"A what?"

"Yes, a club foot," as I drag it behind my body after standing up.

Suddenly it occurs to me, much like when I would write book reports senior year, the meaning of the title. Of Human Bondage.

Slightly raising one brow, Mama lies back down and tucks her feet up and pulls the blanket over her little toes.

A strange bird, I am. Better than, than a dolphin caught in the rapture of a very special sort of Summer Bondage.

Two and Three, Five Altogether

It was shortly after 9 pm Thursday evening. The sun had not fully set and the sky dropped a gray-blue haze over the dinner table on the upstairs balcony. Anatolios and Patricia were having the mousaka that his wife, Chara had made prior to taking off to Athens. A gift of condolence it seems, for Patricia and her new found disability.

Kostas had broken apart his bread and it seeped in the thick rich juice of his vasoolaki. He moved it around with his fork and moaned with joy and gusto as he neared his last full bite, "Bravo Patricia, Bravo."

It was the last meal she had made in good health. A good piece of kitchen magic it was; there was no scrimping on goods or labor. After pulling, clipping and trimming the beans, she had diligently cut up full heads of parsley and dill, three pungent onions, olive oil, and a good dose of chopped mint into the tomato-based string bean stew. The meat she had carefully picked. Savored in the sauce, it was melt-in-your-mouth tender. Certainly, not a bad leftover meal.

Anatolios' cell phone played its familiar tune and as is his favorite pastime, he answered like only this doctor could, perhaps a little bit more animated after his second shot of ouzo. Little was said before he passed the phone across the table to his brother, Kostas, who carefully wiped his mouth and fingers before taking the phone.

"Yasou Alexis," Kostas answered, and with great affection gave the normal "Hi, how do you do?" greeting, laying out the full facts of the previous day's drama. Kostas spoke in Greek of course, but it was in his tongue, and his manner, and it was a story Patricia knew first hand, so her comprehension of his tale describing the previous day's mishap was clear. Emphasis was on his point of view however, which until Kostas had unfolded the story to his younger brother, she had failed to appreciate. As he was winding up, he ended with "Duo kei tria, pente allo mazi." (Two and three, five altogether.)

The numbers, the repeated phrase, made her wounds pang all over again, and now it knocked down her spirit too, as Kostas passed her the phone.

Alex, "Alexis" was a good man, good brother, good husband. Like Kostas, he understood people, men and women well. He is a professional singer in the island circuit, predominantly and most recently on the island of Crete where nightclubs with live performers are abundant and very popular.

Early this year, Alexis had run into some very bad luck. As streets are often overcrowded, with one way this and restricted that, and limited parking, Vespas and motorcycles are the norm for travel. So Alexis was on his way to work early one evening, and the traffic was jammed in front and back. Wheels turned, brakes screeched and he was smacked in the side, breaking his leg. Time heals all wounds, though the waiting is always terrible and longer when we're not young. Time and physical therapy brought him enough health to get back to work, and he was more than glad for that.

Patricia and Alexis had a unique manner of criss-cross communication and understanding; the last five years had been just by telephone. They spoke each other's respective primary languages on approximately equal terms, so their conversations were always broken with she attempting the Greek and he the English, always with affectionate chuck-chuckles in between.

A couple of days after Patricia and Kostas had first arrived in this family's hometown, Alex had called. She had not had the opportunity to speak with him since his accident, and now that he had made it back to work and so was on the mend, she felt the need to hit her brother-in-law with a shot of humor. After the brothers had shared their first "How do you do's?" Patricia spoke into the phone, "Yasou athlefos mou. Ti pragma si eisai? Si einai mia moraki, nei?" (Riding some motorcycle like some little kid?)

Now what she says and what she thinks she says, especially in Greek, are undoubtedly two very different things. Yet, she always speaks in Greek forcibly, with enough confidence to make one listen whether or not her meanings remain true, or her clichés transfer properly.

"Hello my brother. What thing have you? You some kind of baby?"

His reply was with an exasperated sigh and then chuckle, "Ahhhh Patricia, forever young, heh?"

They shared a couple of "How do you do's?" and she passed the phone away.

But today, the shoe was on the other foot. She was the one in need of mercy as she spoke into the receiver; a gentle, wounded voice this time. "Yasou Alexis."

"AAAAAh Patricia," he said with animated concern and long sigh. "How can this be?"

"Nei athelfos." She replied with heaviness. "Hah. Kalo kalokeri, heh?" she replied with a phoney laugh and then less sarcastic grunt. (Yes brother, Good summer heh?)

"What happened? Oh never mind." he resigns, not wanting to extend the pain.

"Ne, einaia kaki matia althelfos mou. Afti kaki matia." (Yes, it's bad eyes, my brother. Those bad eyes.)

"Yes." He affirmed. "Beautiful woman. Beautiful and happy. Always happy, very happy and then Kostas. Hmmm eh, well?" he sang with finality in a "There you have it," sort of manner. Patricia hummed in agreement then handed the phone to Anatolios.

She stood up and piled the plates onto the tray and summoned to the kitchen for help. She carefully followed, limping and pointing to the small counter next to the sink where she organizes the dishes for a pre-rinse, but then hobbled into the bedroom. There she threw herself on the bed, propping her foot on a pillow, whimpering as her eyes filled with tears.

Not a minute had passed and phone chirped again. This time it was Phoebe, Alexis's wife, insisting to talk with Patricia. Unlike her husband of few words, Phoebe knows no English and talks a lot and quickly. So Patricia had to reframe herself, think and speak only in Greek. She spilled out the facts as best she could much to her sister-in-law's loud, compassionate cries of understanding and sympathy. "Duo kei tria, pente allo mazi."

This sister's sighs were just enough to pummel Patricia further into her abyss of despair for a ruined summer. After the call finished, she rolled over on the bed and in Mouille behavior learned from her own mother, slammed her fists into and out of the pillow. Letting out the emotion, she cried like a baby.

The eventful day, Wednesday, the thirteenth of June, started in the now usual fashion, with a late morning rise to head to the beach, beach, beaches...

The first half of June is always questionable. The weather seems and is warm enough, but the clouds come and go and it's near impossible to plan a solid full day until it arrives. One never knows if the white fluffs that contrast the sky will buckle over into gray and let go a summer downpour. Nonetheless, it is preferable to when the kids are all out of school and the unbearable, hot humidity of late July and August. You give, you get.

Either way, the views from the seaside cafes are always awesome and can consume the day with or without the romps into and out of the water.

"Koriche Thele Thalasa" is a song that Mama sung to Patricia many years ago, and it is absolutely true: THE GIRL LOVES THE SEA.

Each morning, late morning, Patricia wakes up and in these years, it's #40 sunscreen. She carefully rubs it all over her body. She doesn't scrimp the cost or the cover all. It's the protection and smooth application she seeks. Then, under her cotton, pocketed after-swim dress, she has on her morning swimsuit. She has three of them. All with different backs and front cut-outs for varying tan lines, all costly, hard to find, one piece, with modesty a must, adequate sure coverage of her voluminous cleavage, mandatory.

After she covers her body with lotion, she packs the beach bag: a little sack of underclothes, another swimsuit for the afternoon dippings with a zip-lock bag to hold the one it replaces when its just too wet to scoot. Then there's another inner sack that holds her Lancome #40, lipstick, wide tooth comb, earplugs in a case, and the novel du jour–which, after finishing up her first three of this summer, is the 495 page *Clan of the Cave Bear*s. Voilá. There you have it. A day in the life of the Koriche Thele Thalasa.

The sky was certainly questionable as they darted through the Katerini neighborhood traffic, on out to the road leading to the beaches. Passing buildings filled with stories of commerce and homes, Patricia grabbed for her book instead of the view. Kostas questioned her about what was happening in this, her current novel. He found it very difficult to believe that this smart tax lady, businesswoman, wife of his, would be humoring herself in the pages of a very thick book about cave bears and their fee fi foes. She felt the same way, but engrossed she was. And so she told him of the escapades of the blonde hair blue-eyed Ayla among the bears and their caves, as they bustled into Katerini Paralia. (The beach.)

A new phenomenon appeared this year. The town had cut off the beach frontage road to all but business delivery traffic and police ticketed any car parked on it. It made the foot traffic and promenades much more pleasant and seemed to increase commerce, but the loss of a half mile on both sides made parking a true chore.

But Kostas found a wee spot in front of one of the many fur shops on the second street up, much to the dismay of the girls who sit at the table outside drinking coffee and blowing smoke at their furs.

He clipped open the back hatch and he grabbed the hats and straw meshed beach chair covers. Patricia grabbed her carefully packed bag, smiled of wonder and said, "You know, I haven't even noticed my foot. I've no problems, whatsoever this summer. Here or in Leptokaria."

"Why in the hell would she bring that up?" he thought, and as a superstitious sign of good measure, reached and knocked on the top of car with his fist as though it were wood.

Patricia has had very little injury in her life and never, knock on wood, a broken bone, that is until two summers ago. Still on the high of another fab six-week Greek and Paris vacation she was walking from her office to the post office when the velcro of her sandal gave way. Her right foot went forward and the back strap held as the sandal wrapped around her ankle tripping her down to the asphalt.

She strapped up the shoe and resumed her walk, and hobbled back to her office in pain noting a bone poking out the side of her foot. Her first broken bone; right small metatarsal. Six weeks in a walking boot and the first trip to Marin General Emergency Room since she was 14, wow, that's seems so many years ago.

Yesterday, the afternoon sun in Leptokaria had not been adequate to fully dry her swimsuit so she had to change out of it still wet. Further, the clouds came and it wasn't until the drive home in the full heat of the car that she was able to shake the chill from her near hour last swim of the day in the deep clear cool crisp sea.

There's practically nothing worse than a cold or the threat of one so early in the vacation, so today she was particularly concerned with the questionable sky. She held back, letting Kostas take his dip first. She was glad for it, as the overcast let go a sprinkle then another as the exodus of beach goers commenced until within minutes the shore was nearly empty.

The rain was light and short. The sky cleared almost completely and the sun was warm when she looked at him, nodded and headed to the water just 20 minutes later.

How exciting it was. Just about 1 pm, the beach and sea almost completely deserted. She threw down her straw mat on the chair and opened her small bag, took out the little blue container that housed the plugs.

Patricia walked down to the waters edge, put her feetsies in the water, twisted the plugs in her ears, stretched her arms and waded up to her shins.

Now the beach at Katerini is a sandy one. There are man-made rock piers that stretch nearly 50 yards out, with at least 250 feet between them making for about six separate beaches. When the water is a bit choppy these piers serve to break the waves making Katerini Paralia–a favorite in Northern Greece, main.

The water has three different levels. It has a gradual decline going out some 35 feet that only goes hip high at its deepest, then dips deeper making it ideal for mothers watching children, or adults that simply can't swim. After that, the sea floor goes up once again to a shin level then gradually, very gradually gets deeper and deeper, only getting over your head the last 10 feet or so, toward the end of the piers.

The beach practically her own, Patricia takes the full liberty of her style. She prefers making her first swim of the day the most athletic, hoping to fend off the lingering results of such good, rich and plenty food. With the water so shallow to start, then again later on, she takes great joy in her buoy ability to skim the tops like an alligator.

She surface dives into the water and then immediately flips onto her back and commences kicking her feet and legs in a bicycling motion with knees up, arms casually at her side to a count of 100. Her muscles open up ever so lightly, pushing her arms back to keep from reaching the second level until 95, 96, 97, 98, 99, "AHHHHHHHH," there it is. She flips onto her tummy there at the second level, straightens her arms down and holds her palms to the sand and starts a count of 50 swish-swish-flutter straight leg kicks. Then after that, she skims the just twenty inches deep water in a froggy, water-skeeter breast stroke, skimming out to sea as the water gets deeper and deeper.

She starts her standing-up water aerobics routine with a strong jog, knees up, fists up and down, facing out to sea. Count 100. Next, 50 jumping jacks with alternate legs going up right and left as far up as she can. Heart's a-beating now in good rhythm, so then it's the rocking horse. Knee up in a corner bend forward, left and same rocking motion with the other leg back, arms in a natural row. Left foot up and hits down and "OWWWWWWWWWWWWW," she spasms up and quickly back down and "OOOOOOOHH AHHHHH, what's that?" Yikes. Uh oh.

She stops the motion and lifts up her foot, the sole nearly parallel to the sky. "Ayee, dang, shit," she looks and what's that piercing through the bottom of her foot?

She can't bear to look, just knows it's bad, it's really, really bad. Quickly she dives forward towards the shore, crawl swimming as fast as she can. As she gets to the second level she hops stands on one foot motioning her arms for Kostas to see. He waves hello back. Ohhhh damn, she looks down and blood is streaming from her foot. She dives forward again knowing she has to bobble on top and stroke faster, faster as fast as she can to the shore.

There she pulls herself up by her arms, twists around putting her rump on the beach. Still in the water. "Kostas, come here, come here." She cries, but softly, trying to camouflage her complete and utter fear and not gather attention. As he comes darting forward he recognizes the grief in her face knowing something is truly wrong.

She's crossed her left ankle on her right knee twisting the

bottom of her foot up. He immediately sees the danger and the severity of the wound, or is it two? The oyster like inner shell glistens in the sun and water and Patricia's face is yellow and full of fright.

It has to come out, so he reaches in and pinches the shell and pulls it out. "Stay here Baby." he warns and runs up shore to get something to compress and clean it. The wounds, yes there are two, spewing blood out into the water. With every strength she has in her very weakened state she studies the cuts and it's evident from the pain and the glistening that a piece of the shell is still in her foot, in the second, deeper cut.

With all her strengths, including character, she still has a near zero tolerance for pain. "Aye, aye, aye!" she cries more internally than externally, but nevertheless, she's defeated, she's absolutely ready to give in. "Oh my God," she thinks "I'm gonna die." It's over. It's over. This is it. I'm gonna die."

Kostas has come back with a bottle of water and a handful of napkins. "Baby look," she cries. "There's another piece." He's scared to death as well but time has served him. He can't panic or Patricia will completely freak out (like she hadn't already). He reaches in and pinches and with a slight twist and tug pulls the remaining piece out along with what appears to be a bloody tongue of sorts that still clings then flings back into her flesh. Yes, the shell has damaged the interiors. She presses with all her might, her right palm against the wounds. Splish splashing the water up right after. Then straightens her legs and pretends not to see the splotches of blood mingle and mix with the outgoing shore. She lets the salt clean the wound as she gives up half a pint of B positive into the Katerini Sea.

Somehow or another, she's hopped up now to the beach chair with napkins compressed. Kostas with his water and now a Band-Aid that clearly is too small to seal the cuts in the most tender spot of her sole, right below the second and third ball. She puts her thongs on and flip flops up to the table and the wooden floor deck of the café.

The waitress and her friend survey the scene but sit tight dragging their cigarettes at the corner-most table in the rear.

"I'm going to get the car, Baby." Kostas announces, "I'll park it very close, as close as I can."

"No problem." she lies. Although she will most probably survive, she will have to manage somehow before she runs out of blood, blood, blood.

The wet sand was all over her legs and feet as she pulls away the compress and the tongue spews out a fresh fountain of Dracula liquid. She turns to the girls, " Ena, ohi, Theo voutali nero, parakalo." (A, no, two bottles of water please.)

"Nai, nai," the waitress replies, bringing the water. Patricia cleans the cuts and begins serious contemplation of how she will be able to make it to the car. It's at least 40 to 50 steps and that's if he has the balls to park it as close as one can with risk of tow and angry Greek storeowners.

She thinks, "How will I do it? How will I do it? I need to tie the wounds up, stop the flow plus keep the bottom of my foot off the floor. Hmmmmm. Hahhhh. My terry cloth cover up."

That was it. She washed the cuts completely, then hopping on her good foot, held the other up with the top and bottom of the blue cover up. Ignoring the pain as much as this girl could, she yanked the cloth up tightly and yanked and twisted it around and around, then looped it into the arm holes and tied it all together with the hood.

"Wow," she felt quite accomplished. So much so, that by the time Kostas had returned, her bag was repacked, towels rolled up and all she said was, "We owe them for two bottles of water."

She was in her dress and hobbled behind him off the deck of the café and look at that, he did have the balls to park it as close as humanly possible. She knew it was so and was glad of it. Off they went. At this point Patricia was surprisingly contained and it was he who seemed most at odds but he tried to hide it.

"Everything will be fine," he said "We will swim again tomorrow."

"Really? You think so?" She replied, surprised but twinkling with childlike wonder and really, really happy.

"Yes, of course," he answered, but knew it was not so. "But now we'll go to the hospital," he said as gently as possible so not to shake up her fear, though his own was not calmed. Those were, after all, not itty bitty wounds. This girl, after all, had lost a lot of blood.

"Hospital?" She questioned, "How 'bout Anatolios. He's your brother, a doctor. He'll know what to do."

Kostas replied with guarded ease. "He's retired. It's easier just to go to the hospital." He knew full well those cuts required stitches. He knew full well there would be no beach tomorrow. He preyed on her trust and temporary feeling that all was now okay and would be okay as long as she believed it so.

The first sign she got that danger was imminent was when he got easily angered and over-worked at slow-moving street repairs requiring a quick detour.

He swore and got pissed off and then took a series of wrong turns. He once lived here for Christ's sake, his brother's a retired doctor who worked at the hospital, he must know where it is. What's up? Right, left, left, right, dead end, one way, wrong way, flinching, swearing, tooting, honking and then finally a sign.

"Hospital" right there. Down the road to the right and another. "There, there it is," she pointed out, certainly not seeing the sign she was used to seeing in the states.

Kostas jammed up the emergency ramp where a row of old wheel chairs and two orderlies stood, smoking, leaning against the building.

"Here. Get out here...Well, wait." Catching himself he swiftly hopped out of the car and came around her side and opened the door. Firmed up his voice and summoned one of the fellows over with a loud, but respectful gruff.

One of the guys with the chairs came forward as she hobbled out of the car. There was a line of folks in varying conditions in a line in the hall. Kostas would have none of that and demanded that she be taken in directly. And so she was, as a set of massive swinging doors opened up.

"Here, go in here Patricia," he ordered. "I'll go park the car and be right back." He made a quick introduction to the nurses inside and off he went.

How could she explain, describe what she saw on the other side of the doors but ask you to imagine an emergency room of another time, another place. "A kid's camp hospital" might describe it best.

It's not that it was dirty, it wasn't. It just was not modern in any degree, never updated since, hmmm well before Lucy Ricardo. No, 1930's maybe.

And the kiosks, nurses' stations, well there were none. There was an old metal desk to the right and the light bulb on a string hung over it from a high ceiling. The floor was cold and painted cement, a green gray and chipping in places with indented drains that she imagined were sprayed down rather than washed up.

There were three beds in a row with curtains between them but they were, well not necessarily dirty, but of a muddy colored rain coat material and the hems were tattered and not properly mended.

The first bed had a moaning man in it who was dirty, perhaps a field man.

There were two girls. It was clear neither of them could speak any English and certainly the two of them though manning it alone, could not be the only authority in this Emergency Room.

A redhead in a green suit, scrubs, was assisting the farmer on the first bed. The brunette was in a white nurse's outfit that looked like it had been handed down by her grandmother and her hat was askew and certainly not properly sized over an unstyled hairdo. She looked much unsure of herself, but after receiving direction from the redhead instructed in sign language for Patricia to lie down on the adjoining bed.

That wasn't something she was going to do as it was just three feet from this ailing man and plus the paper that's pulled down on the cot hadn't been changed and was still mussed from, she presumed, the previous patient.

Patricia purposefully took the third cot, but just sat on its side facing the other beds and surveying the rest of the room, extremely glad her injury was not so severe.

It was the man, the patient that spoke to her first. "Spraken the dirsck?" He asked smiling showing a corn row of some teeth. Patricia ever so politely but completely ignored him looking to the nurse in her grandmother's dress.

"To andre mou einai elinika. Einai exo." Pointing outside the doors. (My husband is Greek. He's outside.)

The girl came over with a little tiny pad of paper and said, "Anoma, parakalo." (Name, please.)

"Patricia, Patricia Petras" she replied. Of course normally she would spell it out but although Patricia could read Greek she couldn't spell out loud especially as she remembered that a P isn't a P, an R was a P and there were two P's in her name….. No, she didn't have a prayer.

The nurse scribbled down something in Greek symbols perhaps phonetically. Then she asked. "Posa chronos…?" then seemed to remember some English, "Years, how many have you?"

"Fifty" Patricia replied and looking over at the page saw the girl write down 30. This is going well she thought.

The nurse then motioned her to lie down. "Hmmm," Patricia thought, and began to unwrap her foot so she could use the terry cover up to cover her thighs for modesty sakes, plus she presumed somebody would be looking at the wound sooner or later.

On her back she had a whole new perspective. She counted 56 mossy green tiles across the length of the room above what would be the door frames. Nine were intact, the rest chipped or pulled or pulling away from the grout, which had its own peculiar color and texture.

She compared the menagerie of bandages and medical supply stuffs on the wall in front of her to the potpourri mixed office supply drawers and closets at her own office back home. But her goods were behind doors, not out in the open like this, and the shelving units were just as ratchety. Everything was there. Everything, squished, on top, on its side, any and everything goes. And labels all seemed to have a murky green color which made it pleasing to the eye, if you liked looking at split pea soup.

She sighed with a bit of worry and turned her head to the left. Now there was an old woman in a dress that was buttoned up wrong. Her arm was in a sling and she was rather insisting on service to no avail. And a young boy now on the bed where the farmer had been seemed to be unconscious, in and out.

But beyond that, in a room behind the desk, Patricia noticed a flurry of people in, what's this, uniforms? Could they be doctors?

Yes. They had identification tags on and they looked somewhat qualified. One clean looking fellow with clear eyes and a strong dose of self confidence came forward and starting asking the little fellow questions then moved his index finger across the line of vision.

And then Patricia heard the nurse in the white outfit describing her own condition to him, that her husband was outside and she believed they were important people.

The doctor came over. He spoke English. His name was Georgos Papandopsomething. He was young and alert, clean, well kept, an intern with a good degree of experience with a head of clean black shiny curls. He asked what happened. Why was she there? What is her name.

Patricia Petras. Her husband was from Katerini, his brother a retired doctor, Anatolios Petras. She said she was on her vacation. She was swimming in the sea, actually doing aerobics and had stepped on a shell. It went deep. There was blood. She was afraid. Her eyes started to fill with tears.

He looked at her with feigned compassion but true understanding. He was knowledgeable. He was caring. He grabbed a stool with wheels, put on a pair of gloves, sat down and scooted himself over to the end of the bed. "Well, now Patricia, let's have a look."

She winced as he touched the wound. Opened up and switched things around. It hurt. It hurt a lot. Patricia folded over her index finger and bit it as he moved things around, grunted and said, "Hmmmmmm."

Just then a wild haired, green-eyed young doctor came quickly through the swinging doors. He said hello to the other doctor first but it was evident he came in directly to her, and asked "Now is this Patricia? Where are you from, My Patricia?"

As he asked the question, the doctor at her feet stood up and a young male nurse who had flanked the green-eyed doctor through the door was now at her other side, starting to hold her hand as tears really filled her eyes. Now with three men about her, she squirmed and pulled her swimming suit cover up tightly over her upper legs and twisted her right knee inward— suddenly feeling so exposed—and grasped at modesty.

"San Francisco,"she answered.

To which he began, "AAhhhhhhhhhhhhh….Okay. I left my heart…." Then the other two joined in "In San Franciscooooooooooooo." Then the wild one looked at Georgos and confirmed that everything was under control. "Yes." With that he said, "Patricia, I'm here if Georgos doesn't do it, but he's best and I'm going to be right over here," as he danced away.

"My husband is outside. Can we get him in here?" She asked looking at her doctor.

He didn't seem pleased with that request and showed it by talking to her as if she were a child, which at this point is exactly what she felt. "First there's nobody here and now there are three. All ready to help you. I'm sorry, Patricia. We only like patients inside this room. You can see it's not too big. Now

I can go talk to your husband outside, or I can tell you and then talk with him completely once we're through. Tell me, what do you want? Either way it will cost you no Euros."

With that she realized he knew what he was doing and he had this male nurse next to her fondling her arm whispering "It's okay, don't worry".

"No problem. It's fine," she replied. "What's the story?"

"Very well." he said. "The wounds are deep. You require stitches."

"Oooooohhhh," she moaned like a child and the young nurse continued his comforting tickling and whispering.

"Two on the small one and three on the larger." he continued "Two and three, Five altogether."

He continued, "You've been to the dentist? You've had shots for pain? We will do the same. You will feel no pain, well perhaps a little for the shots but I can see you are not happy for pain. I will do my best and Ari here well help you through. What do you say Patricia. Shall I finish the job?"

"Yes, go ahead." she moaned, repositioning her cover up and the young, handsome nurse at her side rubbed her arm in his calming fashion and said, "Don't worry. It won't hurt." and looking down at her legs and attempt to cover up, "Don't worry. You will be fine. Don't worry."

And in minutes, she was. The shots were quick. She felt no pain, merely discomfort. Doctor Georgos announced he was nearly done and she cried, "When can I go swimming again?"

"Swimming, you want to go swimming again?" He asked sarcastically and then replied himself. "No water for one full week."

"A weeeeeek?" she cried.

"Yes, why what were your plans?" He answered.

Gaining her composure she replied, "I'm in Greece to swim." She said holding up her arms. "Well, we're here in Katerini for two more weeks, then another two in Paris."

"Ahhhhhh Parishi, heh? Well don't I feel sorry for you, heh?" he said sarcastically and then added, "Serious, now Patricia. You will have one more good week to swim here in Katerini after you heal one week, then you will be fine for Paris. This, this I promise."

Just then the door swung open and she saw Kostas' head peek in with one furrowed brow across his forehead.

"Ahhhh, my husband." she pointed.

"Very good." said Georgos. "I will speak to him now."

Patricia got herself up with the help of little Ari whose soft voice and touch had helped her through the process. He helped her with a plastic booty to which she requested two extra. "You know," she said, "just in case."

Feeling no pain, she plopped down to her feet and joined Kostas who now stood next to Doctor Georgos, who entered information in a patient journal and wrote out a prescription as he spoke.

Kostas looked much relieved, although the silly Ari continued to ask Patricia personal questions and touch her, to which she had to make a mean face and motion for him to go away. After all, his job was done. She didn't need any marital discord at this point.

A week later, and without being able to swim, of course it's been the hottest seven days of the vacation. She did manage to polish off the cave bear book, read *Catcher in the Rye* in an afternoon and now started yet another novel. She sits there with her foot up on the cushion. There's a certain irony in the chapter of the book she's reading now, *Snow Flower and the Secret Fan*, Chapter III, titled "Footbinding." Got to love it.

Anatolios, the brother and retired doctor, bound her foot again this morning after taking the stitches out. Kostas had told her it wouldn't hurt at all. Perhaps that would have been the case if they weren't using an old pair of Mama's scissors and Patricia's eye brow pluckers, and if Anatolios had the eyesight of young Doctor Georgos.

The melodrama would have been stopped if she hadn't had a tetanus shot when she arrived home from the hospital and, of course, he had alcohol, with which he first cleaned the instruments.

Yesterday Kostas and she had ventured to town, none too attractive though. While folks usually give somewhat bad eye to the nice looking curvy lady with the blonde hair braid and striking blue eyes strolling in pretty shoes and dress with her arm in the proud handsome Greek's, they now show a little pity on Patty.

There she is, gimping along in her white gauze wrap covered by the blue plastic sock in Kostas black beach sandals. Suddenly she feels her age.

First they had gone to the laboratory for Kostas' annual blood tests. Her true purpose for getting so excited about going to town today was to pick up her new glasses. She generally gets a pair a year, and this year she picked out a gorgeous pair of gold trim, "flair" specs.

As they were crossing the street from the lab to the optician,

Kostas noted a sports store. "Baby, lets go here, maybe they have those sport shoes for the water."

They did indeed. Black bottomed ones with light blue and pink trim to match her swimsuits. Good show.

The optician was happy to see them come in as they said they'd be in by Friday and it was now Tuesday. The price of those specs would make his fiscal day.

Patricia put them on and though they were attractive, she didn't feel particularly so, feeling her age and all.After that they had a nice cup of coffee at the sidewalk café. The place was hopping, though of course, she wasn't. Loud music and so very many people with so little to do. Young flesh in little clothes. As far as a spectacle it was, though of course she longed to go to the beach. How she pined to go in the water. Koriche thele thalasa.

Saturday, ten days since the mishap and the drama is nearly a dream, a bad one. She's taken a brand new appreciation for the sea. Her stays in it are longer, never hurried and she smiles a whole lot more, lingering, enjoying. And though at one time she would have thought that putting on shoes to go in the water a strange thing, that's not the case now. In fact, she finds pleasure in wearing them, putting them on, looking down at them, feeling their rubber bottoms push down into the sand.

The little shoes get salty and sandy and need to be rinsed at day's end, just like the swimming suits. And as the sky sets there you see them on the clothesline. Dripping. Drying. Two little shoes hanging on the line right next to three swimming suits. All in a row. Two and Three, Five Altogether.

Little Green Book

She fancies herself a writer, she does, but it takes more than fancy to be so, by Jove, it takes discipline. So this year Patricia has committed herself to write in her journal each and every day of the trip. From May 27th to July 16th she will write, keep a daily journal, a diary of sorts and that's each and every day.

To accommodate the duty she selected a small book of pale green sea foam color and with a leatherette smooth surface of a sort of naugahyde with the impression JACK AND JILL on the cover. To ensure she toted it with her everywhere it was purse sized, about that of a novel or small church missal. It numbered about two hundred, two hundred twenty pages, small perfectly sized lines. The book was held most comfortably in her hand. She would fold her fingers up around it and be content to carry it with her wherever she went along with one of her squiggle top green translucent pens which she clipped to the back.

Patricia didn't put her name and address in the book. She had clearly and surely cut her name and info off from her own business address label and fastened the remaining blank label on the inside of the back jacket. There she had written first names only along with complete phone numbers:

To July 1 Greece	Anatolios cell	#011-30-2935387389
	Mama	#011-30-3510600301
From July 1 France	Sean	#011-331-465344920
	Margo	#011-33-5487749207

On the last page she had printed her complete travel itinerary with times, dates and flight numbers. On the page before that she would list all card charges whether it be Euros, dollar amount and vendor.

On last year's trip, although she had read a lot (that is eight books) she hadn't written a word. After a long bout of age related sickness, her husband's mother had passed away just two months prior to their arriving in Greece. The mood and spirit was somber. The emptiness in Mama's home, just the floor below their vacation dwelling, didn't add to her ability to see humor in every day situations.

Patricia would make this year completely different. She would see fun and humor in everything. What's more she would write it all down. She would attempt to do that which she had never even tried. Quite the accomplished baker, maker, cooker of Greek cuisine and upon multiple requests, she would record the recipes she had learned watching and imitating Mama for some 25 years now. None of these recipes are known to others. Mama didn't allow others in her kitchen; she followed no books, wrote nothing down, chop, chop, slice, slice, just a pinch of this and dash of that, scoop of this, cup of that. She'd sniff the jars to figure what was in them: there were no labels here and, of course, you'd only hear Greek vocabulary come from her lips, so making shopping lists for her American protégé was quite indeed, a chore.

There's a strong sensual and sexual side to Patricia that she also wished to record. She promised to bring that out, to "think dirty" and to record on daily basis either fun and fantastic fantasy or folly facts of sexual encounter and intrigue. To help whet her appetite in this regard, her summer reading selection included the French erotica writer, Anais Nin.

Arriving in Frankfurt, it was the layover at the airport that first made her chuckle enough to make her initial "Little Green Book" entry. It was at the airport Starbucks, an international phenomenon where she was to have her first German wish for a green tea latte.

Perhaps it was because she hadn't gotten enough sleep or even too much, but she felt a bit in the Twilight Zone....One, two, three, four, she counted sixteen persons in the general vicinity who were forever looking at their cell phones, putting them away, pulling them back out and ding, dong, ding, no ring, just looking, putting away and then looking again in a most mechanical manner. Patricia went about describing each party in very specific detail, their faces, their bodies, expressions, attitudes, companions what they might be thinking or where they might be traveling. It was quite fun and in addition to keeping her busy until relocating to the gate that would lead to their next destination, served a funny story to break ground in the little green book.

It was a bit funny how she began and then continued to make that little book her mainstay companion, part of everything she did and everywhere she went. If she went out with her handbag, it was in it. If not, she would tote it. To the beach, which was at least twice daily, it lay in her large zip lock bag next to her comb and book du jour that held the smaller inner zip lock that forever carried lip gloss, sunscreen and earplugs. In the car that bag was with her in the front seat. At the beach it was on the table, next to her chair under the umbrella if it wasn't under her pen that was scratching away an adventure or hopeful observation.

Back at home, she was much more personal with it. From the time she came home from the beach, it went down the elevator with her and resided on the coffee table at Mama's. Patricia spent most of her time downstairs alone either in the kitchen, where she cooked all the meals, or in private time with her feet on the coffee table, her back in the chair, her nose in a book or her pen gliding through the pages of the fine lined little green book.

She spotted and then made it her own, a nearly untouched big bottle of ouzo under the kitchen sink. It was that bottle, a little tiny shot at a time, that inspired most of her naughty entries. With exception of three pages of reasons why one might wish her to be naked under her dress or another about her nasty and violent relationship with the sea, most of these daily writings were short, oh my goodness or badness, and embarrassingly to the point. They made her warm to write them down and kept her thoughts as hot as the weather. These tidbits were entered under a separate section two thirds of the way into the book as she was uncertain whether they could be considered suitable for general consumption…..from a Greek Rap song that ended with a peewee girl singing in English "I like it like dis, I like it like dat, I like it like dis, I like it like dat….dis, dat, dis, dat.

It takes a special kind of patience for a really good cook to write down a recipe. One who doesn't know would think you could just sit yourself down and write it all out. They would be wrong. There's no thinking, at least not in a permanent sense when one goes about cooking a fabulous dish. It's an instinctual art but, by golly, Patricia had put her mind to writing down the facts.

It was really tough. For example, when she made the Vasoolaki, is that a pound or kilo of fresh green beans? Cut and chopped, how much is a bunch of dill, mint, parsley? How do you describe how one goes about stripping the herbs from the stalk? How much tomato paste is that glunk you swat in there?

For the Chicken Bay recipe, let's see is that 5 or 7 onions you reduce in 1/3 or 2/3's cup olive oil. And how long does that really take? And once you add the chicken and brown it, how much longer do you wait before adding the bay leaves, the tomato paste, the potatoes? How long is she really out there, sipping ouzo while the dang thing cooks?

Yes, the writing of it down slowed her process quite a bit, but she was truly pleased with the work's results. All recipes were in chronological order as prepared and written within the text of her daily journal entries. Let's see, while certainly not her complete Greek Cooking repertoire, here are the recipes she meticulously recorded:

Spanakotiropita	Spinach Cheese Pie
Vasoolaki	String Bean Stew
Tzasiki	Cucumber Garlic Yogurt Salad
Tiropitaki	Little Cheese Pies
Gemistes Pepperias	Stuffed Bell Peppers

Melgenie Salada	Eggplant Dip
Kota Dafni	Chicken Bay
Souchighakia	Garlic Meatsteak
Horta	Green Horta Vegetable Salad
Pepperias kei Melgenies	Sweet Peppers and Eggplant
Gavros	Fried Baby Sardines

The final Greek story entry to the book was made at Vasiliki's house. Patricia and Kostas had arrived to drop off the Fiat for yet another year the day prior to their departure for Paris. Georgos had come to retrieve them and tote them back to the Hotel Queen Olga in Thessaloniki where they would stay their final night in Greece. The three Greeks sat on the back balcony sharing stories of the outrageous economy as Patricia stepped away inside and pulled out the little green book from her handbag. There she put the finishing touches on the story of the beach encounter of two days before. A band of rude and outrageous Bulgarian girl sun dwellers attempted to oust Patricia from her beach lounge chair and umbrellas. Hah. Like that was going to happen. Nonetheless the silly facts of the tete a tetes made for an interesting read. She chuckled out loud as she recalled then recorded and read over her words of the folly.

Back at Hotel Olga, the book was put to rest as Georgos and Foola were to take Patricia and her husband to a late dinner, then early to rise, well at least for them. Early the next morning, she pulled her pressed shirt from the clear bag in which it had come back from the cleaners. To that sack, she added the new novel that she had decided to read next, along with a comb and her little green book, all of which she would carry onto the airplane. On the way downstairs to check out, she passed the hotel maid's cart. She reached in and grabbed a handful of Queen Olga matches and 2 sewing kits and deposited them in the little see-through sack with the novel, comb and little green book.

They were the last in a big long line at the Cypress Airlines counter to Paris and what with the Greeks butting in from all sides, well it seemed they would remain forever at the end of the line. Always prepared for such atrocities, there were two hours leeway and so not much genuine concern, just impatience brewed.

After the luggage had been checked in, Patricia followed her husband to the carry-on security and passport checkpoint. She removed her belt and placed it with her handbag and plastic pouch full of goodies into the plastic box to go through x-ray. Without a snag, only Kostas' luggage was questioned, as he had a pair of nail clippers that the gal let through.

There were plenty of seats in the internal waiting area as they proceeded to Duty Free to get Dominique her annual bottle of ouzo. Last year we had buffooned and bought the bottle in town. Security had confiscated it at the gate so it was necessary to avoid that kind of conflict and disappointment. Kostas bought it and held the sack right along with his carry-on out past the really comfortable seats that were reserved for smokers, and out to the main waiting area.

All connected to each other, the seats are six in a row with a short table between two chairs on the left and four on the right. Across from those, facing each other is another row of six seats. He deposited his carry-on and ouzo on the chair next to hers while he went to get some coffee and water. Patricia held her purse but put her sack with the books and Queen Olga stuffs on the table by her side. As he arrived back with a little tray she had had to move the sack further aside and he moved his carry-on and ouzo to the chairs across his own. They snacked on the spanakotiropita she had made and packed for the trip and they quite enjoyed themselves. She munched and sipped as she gathered information for a new story.

There were three generations of a Greek family who sat kitty corner, on the other side of Patricia and a row further. It seemed all the packs and carry-ons of the family were put in the care of yaya, grandma, that is. There she sat reading a picture magazine with two or three backpacks on the table next to her and two small suitcases on the two seats on her other side. Her grandson with a moosey hairstyle sat with a friend behind her row pretending not to know her. Her OMG, my-life-is-so-tough, 15 to 16 year old granddaughter sat across from her on the other side of the table from Patricia. She had hollered something at her grandma who continued to occupy that oh-so-awful-airport waiting time with the magazine.

It was evident that gram was practiced at not being affected by either of her grandchildren's bored and plain weird personalities. And so smack, smack, smack, the little girl poop slaps the backside of granma's paper pushing it down to the floor and rattles in Greek in a most snotty and disrespectful tone, "I told you FIVE times, FIVE times, Five times to hand me my backpack!" The grandmother finally looks up only after her daughter, the mother of this most impertinent teenager, enters her zone.

Though Greeks have been cramming the boarding line for a while, just then the Cypress Airline representative announces that the flight would begin boarding the buses that would lead to the aircraft. This gave Patricia her last opportunity to run to the bathroom, which she did. She took a few extra minutes to primp so that when she returned to their seats, Kostas stood up, and asked "You ready?"

"Yes, I suppose so." she replied. And so he reached over and picked up his carry-on and as he reached for the duty free bag she said, "I'll get the ouzo." And so with her purse in one, she grabbed the bottle with the other hand and they headed to the gate.

They were in the last bus and the last group to board. Up the stairs to the plane, and it was very hot. The passengers were tense and heated, all trying to figure out the fan system and the few who were not bath crazy had stolen the air with their sweat.

As the crew closed the doors and began directing all to fasten their seatbelts, Patricia's heart skipped a beat. "Oh my God," she thought, "My bag, my little green book, I've left it!!"

Now she repeats to Kostas "Oh my God, my bag, my little green book, I've left it on the table, in the airport next to our seats."

"What?" He asked angrily, "My God, Patricia." First he let go his total disdain, but then responding to the knowledge that she had put a whole summer's work into the book, he got up and dashed to the head steward and persisted. The steward called in, but it was just too late. Nothing could be done. The plane taxied to the runway for takeoff to Paris and her Little Green Book was left behind.